s.

Great Western Railway Road Vehicles

Bill Aldridge
&
Alan Earnshaw

Trans-Pennine Publishing

CONTENTS

Front Cover: *This 3-ton Scammell Mechanical Horse has been restored into GWR livery and is used regularly at Chappel and Wakes Colne station.*

Rear Cover Top: *The use of articulated trailers was well established by the time this Bedford OSS entered service in 1944. The use of a variety of trailers meant that the railways could carry a multitude of different goods.*

Rear Cover Bottom: *Seen in a sorry-looking state in a Shrewsbury scrapyard, this GWR Thornycroft Nippy was destined to be restored by the Severn Valley Railway.*

Title Page: *Early use of motorised transport by a permanent way team at St. Columb near Newquay in Cornwall.*

This Page: *Acetylene lamps and tarpaulin covers for the driver were the order of the day as late as 1926, as seen on this 30cwt (1.5-ton) van-bodied Burford which probably started life as a bus.*

Right: *Despite the varying styles depicted here at Slough, the four buses on the right all have the Milnes Daimler chassis in common. The bus on the left is a one-man-operated front entrance double decker built on a Straker Squire chassis!*

ISBN 0-9521070-5-8
British Cataloguing in Publication Data
A catalogue record for this book is available from the British Library

The **Nostalgia Road** Series ™
is conceived, designed and published
by

Trans-Pennine Publishing Ltd.
PO Box 10
Appleby-in-Westmorland
Cumbria, CA16 6FA
Tel. 017683 51053
Fax. 017683 53558
ISDN. 017683 53684
e-mail trans.pennine@virgin.net
(A Quality Guild registered company)

Reprographics
Barnabus Design & Repro
Threemilestone, Truro
Cornwall, TR4 9AN
01872 241185

And Printed in Cumbria by
Kent Valley Colour Printers Ltd.
Shap Road Industrial Estate
Kendal, Cumbria LA9 6NZ
01539 741344

INTRODUCTION

Following the highly successful **Nostalgia Road** book, *British Railways Road Vehicles 1948-68*, we now continue our series of books on railway-owned road vehicles. This current title, published exclusively by Trans-Pennine, is the first of a short series of books covering the revenue-earning road vehicles operated by the 'Big Four' railway companies, the Great Western (GWR), the Southern (SR), the London Midland & Scottish (LMS) and the London & North Eastern Railway (LNER). Each of the planned books will take an overall view of the particular railway's road vehicle operation, but as these operations became more and more standardised through the 'Big Four' companies the resulting books could easily become repetitious. Accordingly Bill Aldridge and myself decided that, in addition to the basic story, we would concentrate on some of the more special or unique areas of a particular company's operation or its own viewpoint on the subject. For instance this volume gives much more coverage to the early bus services.

It has often been called God's Wonderful Railway, but the GWR operated far more than just railways. At the time of its demise in December 1947, the GWR operated a massive range of ancillary services. It owned hotels, docks, canals, steamships, ferry services, aircraft, and a massive fleet of road vehicles. Unlike the other companies brought about by the formation of the 'Big Four' railways in 1923, (which were an amalgamation of several large railways within each group), the GWR was a much more different affair.

There had been a Great Western Railway since it was incorporated by Act of Parliament on 31st August 1835, and from the outset the railway had been dependent on road vehicles. This might be illustrated by the fact, that after the opening of the first section of the London - Bristol line (between Paddington and Maidenhead), privately owned road vehicles were conveyed on flat trucks in passenger trains. On reaching their designated station, passengers would alight and their road vehicles were then made ready to take them on to their final destination.

During the building of the Box Tunnel in 1840, road vehicles were used to provide a connecting service for both passengers and parcels between the sections of railway line. Even before the line was opened, a carrier called A.J. Drew saw the potential of linking his road cartage services with the new railway. In August 1839 the first regular goods train ran between Paddington and Twyford, and in addition to general merchandise trucks it also conveyed carrier's road vans on flat trucks. When the GWR finally appointed its very first goods manager, the man they chose for the job was a road haulier, in fact it was none other than the aforementioned Mr. Drew.

Eighty years later, when the Grouping was promoted by the Government as a solution to the problems affecting Britain's railways after World War I, the GWR was already a large company. None of those that it merged with were of any significant size, and thus the GWR's name, and to a large extent its policies, were perpetuated in the new group. There was little real change in management too, and unlike the other groups, there was little of the 'in-fighting' that went on between senior management from the different pre-Grouped railways. In the GWR everyone seemed to pull together, and this undoubtedly affected its forward-thinking policy; not least in the development of services that were peripheral to the main business of running trains. In many ways the GWR was a law unto itself and always seemed to work on the principle of what

ever was good for them should be implemented as quickly as possible. The same ideas were often copied by the other railways, but the GWR did not take unkindly to imitation, as long as they got the credit! In respects to road transport the GWR had many firsts to its name including (in 1835) tentative arrangements with the steam bus operator Hancock to extend his bus service to the newly opened railway terminus at Paddington.

This was followed by a series of 'firsts', including the first petrol bus, the first petrol lorry, the first railway-owned battery-powered lorry, and several other innovations. Many other new ideas and schemes came about during the reign of the Paddington management and these will be described in the text. It is the story of this progress that we now begin to chart. It is also a story that has been told before, and many readers may have seen the excellent volumes on Great Western Railway vehicles published by OPC some years ago. However, we make no excuse for addressing the subject once again from a different angle, and this volume is meant to be complementary to those editions by concentrating more on the operation of the vehicles involved.

Below: *This Ford Model A platform bodied truck worked from Shrewsbury Station, in an area shared by the GWR and the LMS hence the LMS Express Parcels van in the background.*

THE EARLY DAYS.

The early railway promoters apparently placed little emphasis on the need to offer road feeder services for goods, after all the very first railways were largely mineral lines designed to take goods from the mines and quarries of Great Britain to docks, harbours, navigable rivers or canals. The most typical example of this is the Stockton & Darlington Railway of 1825, which was designed only to handle train loads of coal and frankly found all other sources of traffic an embarrassment. By the time the Liverpool & Manchester Railway opened five years later, the idea of single wagon loads was found to be a lucrative business. Then came the less than wagon load traffic, where the goods of different customers were made up in 'destination' wagons, which again was found to be even more profitable as higher rates could be charged.

Even so the concept was still station to station, but railways began to build warehouses and goods delivery yards, where this assorted traffic could be handled or forwarded to another destination. On the Liverpool & Manchester a huge warehouse was built in a matter of weeks at the Manchester terminus to handle, sort and store this 'less than train load' traffic.

Above: *A lovely photo of the Yorkshire steamer operating on the Stanford on Teme goods service. The 4-wheel trailer had its own set of brakes operated by the second man sat on the trailer.*

Other railways quickly imitated the concept, including the Bristol & Exeter Railway which later became an important part of the GWR. However, in the main it was the long-suffering customer who had to arrange collection of the goods from the nearest goods yard or warehouse. The alternative was for a company to build their factories and warehouses alongside a railway line, either buying or leasing land from the railway company concerned. Once established, a 'private delivery siding' agreement would be signed, and the business was provided with a connection to the railway network.

These private delivery sidings varied from a short single spur into the works, to a complex internal railway network. In both instances railway company wagons could enter the premises, and many enterprising firms (especially the larger ones) owned or leased their own fleet of rail vehicles. Whilst this situation may well have been suitable for firms willing to relocate and invest in rail connection, it did little for those customers who had well-established premises that were not geographically suited for rail connection.

Above: *This unidentified location shows a typical scene, with a pair of GWR horse-drawn wagons collecting goods from a depot. The amount of goods that these horses would be expected to pull was quite substantial, and may be judged by the height to which one of the wagons in the background is piled. At various locations, where steep banks were encountered leading into or out of the goods yard, 'chain horse teams' would be provided to assist with banking or braking wagon teams as they ascended or descended.* The late-David Cantrell Collection

Below: *The quay at Weymouth provides the backdrop for this atmospheric view of horse-vans awaiting His Majesty's Mails and other more prosaic parcels being off-loaded from the Channel Island steamer.* The late-David Cantrell Collection

The PDS arrangement also did very little for the growing retail trade, the small manufacturer with their restricted finances, or the large agricultural industry in Britain. All of these had to employ horse and carts to provide a link to the rail head, which by reasons of geography might be several miles away, and this could hardly be considered as an acceptable level of service.

This was a changing time in Britain, as it moved from being an agrarian society to an industrial one, and the railways fuelled the process of change. People migrated to the towns and cities in search of the 'new' employment, and the country had to supply the needs of these new industrial communities with produce and food. In turn the industrial areas supplied the country with mechanisation and improved consumer commodities, and thus a flow of different types of traffic developed. The canals, packhorses and stagecoaches had previously handled some of this, but the railways were soon to become the primary carrier. Accordingly it became more and more necessary for the railways to be able to offer a greatly enhanced level of service, and this then spawned the construction of new branch and secondary lines to feed traffics to and from the main lines.

Once the railway network had begun to be established, then the operators began to look at the ways they could expand into the hinterland surrounding their rail routes. In some instances further branch lines were the answer, but more often than not a collection and delivery service for parcels and goods traffic would adequately suffice the expectations of the time.

In common with all the major main line railways, the GWR's first foray into the road movement of goods was to offer a service carrying passengers' luggage door to door. This was a great success, and it soon expanded into other types of small traffic carried in both passenger trains and freight trains. This movement of goods became known as cartage and, as it grew, it was divided into three separate categories, namely; Passenger Parcels, Less Than Wagon Load Traffic and Full Wagon Load Traffic, all of which required a different style of handling.

The initial passenger parcels service made use of handcarts, with porters employed to move reasonable sized items to addresses within a mile radius from the station. This system rapidly became inadequate so horses and carts were employed. Initially two-wheeled traps were used but these were often found to be too light for the growing work at many stations. Before long 4-wheeled drays were in widespread use and thus the GWR could offer an improved service for the movement of heavier parcels over a greater radius from the station. Although the GWR generally liked to operate this service themselves, there were often more pressing uses for the capital expenditure required, especially in areas where the traffic might not be particularly heavy. Where the railway did not operate its own service, a local cartage agent would be employed to carry out the collection service on their behalf. The grandfather of one of your authors was employed as a cartage agent by the Lancashire & Yorkshire Railway until the start of the 1920s, based at the branch line terminus at Meltham near Huddersfield.

These agents were often subsidised by the contracting railway company, but even so this provided the most cost-effective means of offering an 'all inclusive service'. Many of these agents worked from just one station with perhaps just one horse and cart, but there were a number of larger agents who covered relatively big areas. One of these large companies was Pickfords, who became agents for the GWR as long ago as August 1843.

The charging system for the goods carried was initially based on two separate rates, one for the rail journey and one for the road journey. This caused many problems and soon just one rate was charged for each consignment. However, even this scheme was not quite as simple as it sounds since the goods were charged more on their value than weight and even then there were many anomalies in this situation. The biggest long-term problem was the fact that the railway companies were required by law to publish all of the rates charged and this enabled the more enterprising road hauliers to undercut the railway prices. In the long term this was a recipe for disaster, but in the first few decades of this century the railways were the only organisation able to offer a truly nation-wide collection and delivery service for large parcels and goods traffic.

From the outset the agents were vital to the growth of the goods delivery operation and we should not underestimate how extensive this arrangement became. To do this we might give an idea of the size of the cartage agent's operations, not at their peak (when we might expect to see a high figure) but as late as 1932, or a full decade after the Grouping. At the end of 1932 a total of 735 GWR stations offered goods and parcels facilities, and of these 270 were still worked by agencies. Some of these agents remained committed to railway cartage right into the nationalised era. However, in the first decade of the Grouping era, a total of 145 agency operations had already been absorbed into the GWR operation.

For a long time the maximum weight of any one individual item handled by the cartage fleet was restricted by a number of factors. These included:- The availability of high-capacity horse-drawn drays; the inability of lifting gear or cranes to handle heavy weights and, possibly even more important; the lack of good, hard-wearing, road surfaces outside town centres.

Things rapidly began to change in the country areas after the introduction of the traction engine, and with the advent of these engines came improved heavy-duty low-load trailers. This led to heavier loads being handled than had been possible with the horse-drawn vehicles of the day. However, much depended on the skill of the traction engine drivers in extricating their engines from holes in the road or from collapsed road surfaces. Such incidents did lead to an improvement in road engineering, and very gradually the highways and byways began to improve.

As the industrial revolution reached its zenith, the railway's ability to move heavy goods to even the most remote locations had been perfected. In turn more and more new machinery was taken to more and more new factories and this allowed them to produce more and more goods to supply the needs of the Empire.

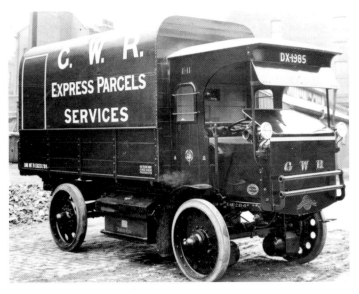

Above: *Although the earliest GWR battery-electric vans dated from 1906 and 1908, no further electric trucks were purchased until 1919. Then models built by General Vehicles of Tyseley (Birmingham) and Ransomes, Sims & Jeffries of Ipswich entered the fleet. The R.S.& J. Orwell electrics featured front wheel drive as seen here at Swindon in 1919.*

Below: *Another London-based truck builder was H. G. Burford and they became a major supplier to the GWR. Their vehicles featured American built components and this 1-ton van dates from 1922. This is, of course, a petrol-engined van and it shows the 'chocolate and cream' coaching livery used on the vans at the time.*

By the turn of the century the GWR was able to offer an extensive collection and delivery network offering diverse services like: 'Passengers-forwarded' parcels (moved in light horse-drawn vehicles, often 2-wheeled vans): Heavier 'smalls' traffic (on horse-drays): Bulky or heavy items such as steel and machinery (by multiple horse team or very occasionally by hired traction engine).

The first real mechanically propelled vehicle used by the GWR was a Thornycroft steam wagon hired from the manufacturers in 1902, which took part in various trials in the Birmingham area. The overall success of these trials proved that the railway company could successfully offer a delivery service based on the use of self-propelled road vehicles and this led directly to the next stage, namely the introduction of petrol-driven vehicles as detailed in the following chapter. Strangely enough despite the publicly announced success of the trial, the Thornycroft was soon returned to the Basingstoke works of its manufacturer. By 1909 the fleet of steam-driven road vehicles numbered just three examples.

The first of these was a Yorkshire waggon working at Worcester on agricultural work for a local Co-operative society. It had been delivered in 1905 and was first put to use along the route of the abandoned Teme Valley railway and was based at Henwick station near Worcester. Its traffic came from the Teme Valley Agricultural Organisation Society and had been known to tow up to three trailers at a time. Despite its early success this service soon faded away. The short life of this early project was no reflection on the quality of the staff or indeed the vehicle, it was just that as the roads in the country areas improved the farmers found it possible to move their own goods. The other two steamers were both Wallis Steevens tractors, which were used at the Bilston Ironworks in Staffordshire.

Top Left: *Always willing to try out vehicles from manufacturers situated within the GWR operating area, the company bought a number of vehicles from Guy Motors at Wolverhampton. This 2-ton van, again with a Swindon-built cab and body dates from 1931.*

Centre Left: *This photograph and the one below feature the Morris Commercial 'T' Type 1-ton van, which was first introduced in 1924 and featured a Hotchkiss type 4-cylinder side valve engine with a clutch using cork inserts running in oil and rear axle brakes only. The upper van may well have been a works demonstrator whilst the lower is the standard GWR vehicle. Both have Morris-designed van bodies though they may have been completed by the GWR. The normal T type van came complete with electric lighting, but the GWR seemed to insist on the well-proved acetylene lighting system.*

Bottom Left: *This view shows a later 1-ton van, this batch of vans was definitely fitted with Swindon-built bodies to a much simpler design. Observant readers will note that in this photograph (and several others used in the book) the vehicle has had its original fleet number crossed out and replaced with a new hand-written number.* Buckinghamshire Railway Centre

THE FIRST MECHANICAL VEHICLES

The accolade of operating the first internal combustion engined vehicle on any of the pre-grouping railway companies also belongs to the GWR, for around the start of the 20th century the company began considering a variety of applications for the operation of light railways. As the name implies, Light Railways were constructed to much 'lighter' standards of engineering and were seen as a means of opening up parts of the countryside that had not been considered economic in the earlier stages of railway development.

The gauge of the light railways could be to any number of variations, but most were standard gauge (4ft 8$\frac{1}{2}$in) and thus they offered a full interchange of traffic with the main railway network. Although the Light Railway Act, passed in 1896, had created the possibility of numerous new schemes within their territory, the GWR were wary of building many of the proposed new lines. The Act had opened a floodgate, and every rural community wanted to have its own line, but the GWR were (quite rightly) unsure of the level of custom that would be generated.

Above: *This is Milnes Daimler Wagonette number 2 about to leave Helston station for the Lizard in 1903. The vehicle had a 4-cylinder engine and the final drive was through noisy external gears.*

As many of these schemes were intended to act as feeders to existing railway lines or stations, the GWR came to the conclusion that it might be possible to operate road vehicles in the first instance. The purpose behind this was to a) assess the likely demand for the service, and b) see if an alternate road service could be operated at a lower cost than building a new rail route.

The passenger feeder services, using a variety of buses proved very popular, even though many communities kept up the pressure on the railways to build a railway branch line into their area. From this very low key beginning, the GWR became the largest operator of railway-owned buses with a network of routes spanning the whole of the railway's operating area, in an era lasting for over a quarter of a century. For the record the first mechanically propelled bus service operated by any railway was a Thornycroft steamer in Ireland in 1902.

Another very early motor omnibus proprietor was Sir George Newnes, who instituted a service between Ilfracombe and Blackmoor in Devon in conjunction with his famous Lynton & Barnstable Railway from June 1903. Unfortunately it became impossible to operate the vehicles on this particular route because the local police issued a summons on the enterprising Baronet and his drivers. Their crime was speeding at the astounding and earth-shattering rate of 8 mph! As a result the buses very soon came to be sold to the forward-thinking GWR. They went back into service on 17th August 1903 between Helston and the Lizard, acting as a feeder to the railway and parallelling the route of a proposed light railway.

The GWR had considered employing an agent or subcontractor to operate this (and other services that they were proposing), but by using their own staff and the second-hand buses to prove this route, they saved themselves an outlay of £85,000 (£5,683,000 at today's prices) for a light railway. The two (almost new) 22-seat buses were Milnes Daimlers fitted with 16hp petrol engines and had been bought along with a Panhard 'car' for the sum of £2,100 (£140,280 today). These first GWR buses actually ran contrary to legal requirements since they weighed over 3$\frac{1}{2}$ tons and required a man to walk in front of them holding a red flag. The problem was quickly resolved by stripping out some equipment and painting 2ton 19cwt (2.95-ton) on the sides! One of the original open vehicles on this route was replaced in November of 1903 by a similar vehicle, but with a fully enclosed body though of lower seating capacity and still able to carry about 15cwt (750kg) of passengers luggage.

Top Left: *Another animated scene at Helston with a Milnes Daimler bus about to depart. The vehicles were not ideal for use on the poor quality roads of that time and the drivers had to act as mechanics quite regularly. The trip to the Lizard Point must have been quite fatiguing for the passengers, but the beauty of the most southerly point in England must have been adequate compensation.*

Centre Left: *This unusual vehicle was known as the 'Jersey Car' and was mainly used on private hire work. It was based on a Milnes Daimler chassis but was built more like a charabanc than a bus and it required a ladder for the passengers to reach up to the rear seats. It is seen here awaiting to depart on a tour from Falmouth Station.*

Bottom Left: *Penzance is the location for this photograph showing the GWR's first double-decker - a Milnes Daimler bus bought for the Marazion, Penzance and Newlyn route. Looking at the capacity load and the crowds this might be the inaugural trip in 1904.*

Top Right: *In the Spring of 1904 a new service was started in the Home Counties linking Beaconsfield and Slough (Buckinghamshire). The bus is Milnes Daimler No.5, which had been originally registered in Cornwall but is photographed here outside the Royal White Hart Hotel in Beaconsfield.*

All photos The late-David Cantrell Collection

The services on the route were suspended from October 1904 to April 1905 however, owing to a dispute with the local council regarding damage to the road surface. The dispute as to whose responsibility it was to repair the road was resolved when the GWR loaned a steamroller to the council.

The Helston venture was deemed very successful however and the company, aware of the need for new services elsewhere, placed an order for a further 25 Milnes Daimler chassis and bodies. These vehicles were based on a German-built chassis and sold by G.F. Milne and Co. of Shropshire who were well known as tramcar builders. The same buses were also extensively used in London and had a successful career prior to World War I.

The drivers of these buses needed to be very skilled since they had to operate three separate change speed levers (two forward one reverse). They also had to keep two glass bottles on the dashboard filled with oil and often pump fuel from the petrol tank if the exhaust driven pressure valve failed! In addition to this the drivers had to handle the regular servicing and breakdown repairs just to keep these early vehicles operational. The vehicles ran on petrol with an added touch of benzole or paraffin and the petrol was sent out in 5-gallon cans from the GWR's central depots to the local outstations.

All of the earliest Milnes Daimlers had rear wooden brake shoes that operated only on the solid tyres themselves, which was less than satisfactory. The GWR works in Swindon soon designed a better braking system, and this was retrospectively fitted to the buses as they came in for major overhauls. When travelling uphill there was always a danger that these vehicles would run backwards so the conductor walked behind, ready to drop a wooden scotch under the rear wheels in case the bus came to an involuntary halt.

The electrical system on these vehicles was very basic, with a magneto supplying current to a non-insulated brass rod for the low-tension sparking plugs which, in turn, incorporated a separate 'make and break' mechanism for each cylinder, actuated from the camshaft. The return springs on these plugs often got lost, so the drivers would collect empty earthenware ginger beer bottles so they could use the rubber rings from the stoppers as improvised springs in case of need. When the new Milnes Daimler vehicles were built two of them appeared at the Commercial Vehicle Show. One of these had a double-deck body, but this was unfortunately too heavy for the chassis and it was soon converted to a single-decker. The first of these new vehicles was put to use in the South West where it was soon followed by a number of others.

Above: *The Clarkson steam buses, like the one shown here, had mixed fortunes before they eventually entered service on the Wolverhampton to Bridgnorth route, but found that the hills were too difficult for them to traverse and these buses got transferred to more equitable routes but even then they never proved reliable.*

Below: *This rather intriguing photograph depicts a Straker Squire chassis prior to being bodied as a bus in 1910. One assumes that the engine in the foreground is for training purposes and the men could be trainee drivers or mechanics. Like many of the views in this book, this picture was found in an old scrapbook at the Slough offices by the late-David Cantrell who had been ordered to destroy several cabinets of old records. Deciding that the photographic images and old postcards in the book were too valuable to throw away, he 'unofficially' retained them - and we are truly glad he did!* Both the late-David Cantrell Collection

By Easter 1904 the company had instituted a small number of tours utilising chassis fitted with a charabanc-style body. A further boost to the passenger road services was the decision of the Post Master General to allow mail to be carried on the buses. Allied to the need to carry freight and passengers luggage, this meant that some of the buses were fitted with mail and/or freight compartments, whilst others had strengthened roofs to enable goods to be carried upstairs. The mail carrying buses could only stop at designated places given in the time bills, whereas the other buses could stop anywhere that was safe to collect passengers. Later that year a proper double-deck bus entered service in Torquay and was soon followed by a similar vehicle working in Windsor.

Also in 1904 one of the buses used on the Lizard service was badly damaged in a fire at its Helston Depot, when its wooden body was completely burnt out. Always a company to find success from misfortune, the GWR had the chassis repaired and it was then given a goods vehicle body and used on a goods collection service in Penzance that commenced in 1905.

The vast majority of chassis purchased up to 1905 had been Milnes Daimler's, but orders also came to be placed for some Clarkson steam buses and Wolseley petrol chassis. One 5-ton Milnes Daimler, bodied from new as a lorry, had the unenviable task of running daily from Paddington with fish (from the South West of England) for sale at Billingsgate the country's foremost fish market. It is a remarkable fact that, as 1904 came to a close the GWR were operating more motor buses than were actually running in London.

To enable even more new routes to be opened during 1905, the company ordered three Straker Squire, 13 Durkopp, and 17 Milnes Daimler chassis. A total of seven buses appeared at the Commercial Show of that year, including a Maudslay that had been ordered earlier. With the exception of the feeble Clarkson steamers, none of the fleet of petrol buses offered any protection for the drivers except for a very high roof, which did no more than trap the inclement weather. This year also saw services extended further into South Wales and Dorset.

Of the vehicles ordered in 1904, five of those from Durkopp were cancelled due to poor delivery and one of the Straker Squire's received a front entry double-deck body suitable for one man operation. This was a real first, since the OMO concept did not take off until the 1970s, however it was short-lived for the body was soon converted to rear entrance following complaints from some lady passengers. This body incidentally was built by G. Scammell & Nephew who later found fame by building Britain's first articulated lorry. One fascinating comment on some of the early double-deckers was that access to the top deck was by a vertical ladder mounted at the rear of the vehicle, which passengers of both sexes would have to ascend! Entrance to the single-deck bodies was generally by rear-mounted steps.

Up to this date all of the buses purchased had been of normal control design, that is with the engine in front of the driver, but some of the Wolseley buses had the driver sitting on top of the engine compartment giving a semi-forward control driving position.

Above: *This Milnes Daimler with Dodson body had been an exhibit at the 1905 Commercial Motor Show and later went on to work in Buckinghamshire.* The late-David Cantrell Collection

Of all of the early chassis designs only the Milnes Daimler vehicles could be said to be reasonably reliable, whilst the Clarkson steamers had a very short life. Furthermore the buses supplied by Durkopp and Wolseley were often out of service and some of the Durkopp vehicles were given replacement Milnes Daimler engines. Actually, the Milnes Daimler's also had problems due to an intriguing drive-line to the rear wheels, which made use of a pinion gear running on an internal gear ring fitted inside each rear wheel.

This system was both so noisy in operation and in need of frequent servicing, that it eventually had to be replaced by a more normal axle. In London the police were in fact very unhappy about the noise that these gears made, but at the time the bus operators could do little to alleviate the problem. On the GWR further second-hand Milnes Daimlers were purchased from the Associated Omnibus Company of London in 1907 following the precedent set in 1903, and these were mainly used to replace the ailing earlier buses.

Just before World War I a total of 15 Maudslay chassis had entered service, carrying both coach and bus bodies and the service was set to expand! However, the GWR were then faced with a really unfair situation, which saw it abandoning several routes following the Government's request for them to discontinue 'non-essential' bus services in the interests of fuel economy.

To their disgust the GWR then found those routes being taken over by independent operators thereby totally negating any overall fuel savings! The buses that were relieved of their duties often came to be converted to lorries, and many of their crews joined the Forces. Because of the number of men 'signing up' during 1916, the GWR was forced to employ women on jobs that had previously been a male preserve. Now women became conductresses on the buses or drivers for both the horse-drawn and motorised parcel vans.

At the road vehicle headquarters in Slough, the company was involved with both making components for the war effort and manufacturing spare parts for the large fleet of Milnes Daimlers, which having many components of German origin were becoming increasingly difficult to replace. To further help the war effort the Slough workshops got involved in the conversion of around half of the fleet to run on coal gas in order to save the precious supplies of petrol. The conversion consisted of a large bag to hold the gas being tied to the vehicle's roof and a mixing apparatus to obtain the correct gas/air mixture.

13

Early Goods Vehicles.

Mention has already been made of the operation of a Milnes Daimler lorry in London which, along with the steamers, clearly highlighted the potential in developing mechanised delivery and collection services. Encouraged by the success of their buses, the GWR ordered two Wolseley chassis in 1904 to carry out further experiments in the haulage of goods by road. Again success was clearly measurable, so the management decided to acquire two battery-electric trucks to test this form of traction.

Above: *One of the very earliest motor powered vehicles owned by the Great Western Railway was this 1904 Milnes Daimler, which was used for the movement of goods in London. One of its regular tasks was transporting fresh fish from Paddington to Billingsgate Market.* The late-David Cantrell Collection

One of these was purchased from the Anglo American Motor Co. whilst the other one was built by the GWR at their Slough workshops, with its general concept being based on the American Riker design.

This experiment shows that the company was forward-thinking enough to try out electric vehicles, and the model built at Slough featured an 80-volt battery and two motors that drove the rear wheels, but as ever with battery-electric vehicles the initial promise was never realised. In fact this was a situation that continued well down into British Railway days, as the management repeatedly tried to find an electric vehicle to employ on its urban delivery work.

With the continuing growth in parcels traffic, in 1908 the company decided to invest in six petrol engined Straker Squire 1-ton chassis and had them bodied as parcels vans at their Swindon works. These vans were placed in service in Birmingham and Birkenhead, which were both busy and thriving areas. The Straker Squire chassis were of German origin, with the importer originally using Bussing chassis, though as time passed the British content of the chassis increased.

In the preceding five years period the passenger road vehicle services had been the major concern of the GWR, yet for the next six years bus services seemed to take a back seat in comparison to the mechanisation and growth of the goods and parcels service. Just six new passenger vehicles entered service in 1910, although the tour services were increased. This situation continued up to the outbreak of World War I, and was a great shame since it enabled a number of other 'private' operators to commence new services. This either restricted the potential areas in which the GWR could 'expand' its passenger services or allowed competitors into areas where they had previously had a complete monopoly. Goods traffic on the other hand was still in the hands of the GWR cartage services (or the agents), but improvements could obviously still be made. Experiments continued, and additions to the road fleet consisted of a further six 1-ton Straker Squire vans and three Auto-Carrier 'vans'. The latter were no more than motorised tricycles with a box van at the front with the driver sitting at the rear over the engine and rear wheel.

The next year, 1911, saw a further 24 Straker Squire vans join the fleet along with a Milnes Daimler van fitted with a proper rear axle, this vehicle later appeared in the guise of a 'hotel bus', carrying passengers for the Treganna Castle Hotel at St. Ives. In fact this process of changing the body of vehicles was commonplace in the early days of road motor operation by the railway. Indeed many of the earlier buses became lorries, whilst others occasionally swapped bodies between goods and passenger during the year aided by the simple straight frame chassis of that era.

Amongst other orders of 1911 was one sent to Commer Cars for five lorry chassis and another to Dennis for some 20hp buses to give a better level of service through their improved power. The GWR also experimented with an American Knox articulated tractor unit which was used in conjunction with three trailers. Despite the success of the goods and parcels operations in London, Slough and Liverpool, the services at Henwick, Penzance and Saltash had to be withdrawn. In contrast new services commenced in West Wales (at New Quay and St. David's) as we will discuss later. All of the services and vehicles noted above, should really be considered as no more than trials with a brand new concept that was in its infancy.

Above: *The GWR decided to experiment with a large, but simple battery-electric truck to see if it would be more reliable than the contemporary petrol vehicles. At the time there were no British manufacturers who could offer such a vehicle, so they turned to America for this model.*

Below: *When the GWR decided to build their own battery-powered delivery vehicle, they only had the American prototype to base their plans on. This truck was built at the GWR Slough workshops in 1908 and although it rarely did so, it could cover 30 miles on one single charge. Both the late-David Cantrell Collection*

Above: *Using a chassis built by the London company of Sidney Straker & Squire, these 15cwt vans had bodies built at Swindon before World War I. An article in the* Commercial Motor *magazine of 1920 described these Straker Squires as 'ancient', how time flies!*

Below: *During the material shortages associated with World War I, many large fleets converted a number of vehicles to operate on coal gas. In this instance the gas is carried in a large roof-mounted bag with the off-take at the rear. As the bag emptied the gas would flow to the rear of the bag, hence the long tube leading to the engine.* Both the late-David Cantrell Collection

Today we take the superiority of the motor vehicle for granted, but in the years leading up to 1914 nothing like that could be assumed. It was quite a step into the dark for a management team who were far more used to steam engines or traditional horse flesh.

Despite some misgivings the GWR obviously deemed the 'trial operations' of internal combustion vehicles a success, and authorised further development. With the road vehicle fleet building up, a headquarters office (with a main overhaul and repair shop) was established at Slough, Buckinghamshire. In total around 100 passenger and 50 goods vehicles were then in service, but it is very difficult to give exact figures due to the dual identity of many of the vehicles as they could be a bus one day and a lorry the next.

By the outbreak of World War I, a total of at least 36 Straker Squire 1-ton parcel vans were in use. These vans were only 13ft 8in long and had the ability to deliver goods to places that were almost inaccessible to other forms of transport! We have described these little vehicles as vans, which was correct as far as the load carrying portion was involved, but the poor driver had to sit in the open with only a front shield and a folding canvas cover (just like a shop blind) for protection.

The periodical *Tramway and Railway World* noted in 1912 that 'these vehicles are fitted with a 2-cylinder 14.4 hp engine with interchangeable mechanically operated valves. Three speeds and reverse are provided with top gear being direct drive and the transmission from the gearbox to the back axle is by cardan shaft and worm and wheel gearing.' The earlier batch of Straker Squire vans had operating costs split as follows;

Petrol	0.45 pence per mile
Oil and grease	0.047 pence per mile
Cleaning materials	0.023 pence per mile
Tyres	0.85 pence per mile
Estimated maintenance	1.00 pence per mile
Total	**2.37 pence per mile.**

In 1914 the railway ordered some 20 Thornycroft parcels vans but, prior to their delivery to the GWR, the War Office commandeered half of these. With the outbreak of war the GWR, along with every other major railway (and most minor ones), came under the control of the Government-controlled Railway Executive Committee on 5th August. As a result of the immediate priority to mobilise the British Expeditionary Force, massive reductions in railway services were ordered. This was to have an impact on both passenger traffic, and also the freight operation. In the first four weeks of the hostilities, some 1,404 journeys were made by the Express Cartage section to collect 'Officer's Luggage (Army)', whilst a further 689 runs were made for 'Officer's Trunks (Navy)'. The normal cartage operation was also very busy, collecting all the essentials of a country readying itself for war. All manner of items were being sent by rail, including no less than 9,000 cases of dubbin from a company in Bristol, and 4,000 chamber pots from a manufacturer in the Black Country.

As a consequence of the extra traffic generated by the hostilities, the GWR had to make immediate alterations to its 'civilian' services. Most notably, as far as the road operation was concerned, it withdrew all of its bus tours and also ceased operation of the various summer-only routes, before bringing in the winter services earlier than normal on the other routes. With this reduction in services, the number of vehicles required for passenger work dropped substantially. As a result a number of the earlier chassis had their bus bodies removed, and lorry bodies then replaced these.

During World War I the railway horse maintained its supremacy on cartage and haulage work, but very large numbers of horses, carts, wagons and drays were requisitioned for military use. Once this dreadful war came thankfully to a close, life gradually began to return to normal. Modernisation, put on hold for over four years, could once again be resumed. With respect to road vehicles, the GWR had now three factors that greatly influenced the process of change. Firstly, much of the material sent to support the troops at the front, including horses and carts, never came back. Secondly, the war itself had brought about a tremendous process of evolution in the motor vehicle, and as a result much more reliable chassis and engines were available. Thirdly, many hundreds of vehicles had been purchased by the British and American forces, and these were now laying in Ordnance Depots around the country surplus to requirement.

As part of its reparation obligations, the War Office allocated numbers or war surplus road vehicles to the railway companies to compensate for the vehicles requisitioned during the period of hostilities. As the Great Western, London & North Western, Midland and Lancashire & Yorkshire railways had supplied the greatest number of vehicles to the military, they were offered the 'lion's share' of the surplus vehicles.

The GWR obtained 108 AEC 'Y Type' lorries from the army, and then ordered an additional 60 direct from the Associated Equipment Company. The 'Y Type' had been built on the famous 'moving production line' at the AEC works in Walthamstow and no less than 10,000 vehicles had been ordered by the Government for use in the war effort. The most astounding feature of this order is the fact that AEC had never built lorries before, but the outstanding reliability of a fleet of their buses (some of which had been requisitioned off the streets of London in 1914 for use as troop transport) led to this order.

Eventually the number of AEC 'Y Type' vehicles in the GWR fleet reached 360, of which some 70 operated as buses. The 'Y Type' was built to carry about 3½ tons and as such was not exactly a lightly-built model, so when some of them came to be used as buses the engineers modified the springing to give the passengers a slightly better ride. Many of these buses had a relatively short life, after more suitable passenger-carrying models came onto the market. The GWR management being sensible businessmen then converted the vehicles back to lorries for a second life. Indeed a number of these vehicles led a double life often having a bus or charabanc body placed on the chassis during the summer, then losing that body to a load carrying platform during the winter.

Above: Is this a commercial vehicle or a public service vehicle? Actually the answer could be yes to both. This amazing beast was originally built as a Milnes Daimler parcels van in 1910, but three years later it was converted into a bus for the carriage of hotel guests at the Treganna Castle Hotel at St. Ives, Cornwall. This was a GWR owned hotel and the bus would transport guests to and from the station and the golf course. A little later a more conventional Thornycroft bus took up this duty. The late-David Cantrell Collection

Below: This Milnes Daimler chassis has been rebuilt and fitted with a new GWR designed radiator. Whether the bus had been involved in an accident and the original design of radiator was no longer available or whether the GWR decided to up-date the image of the vehicle is not known. Alternatively it could have been taken during a conversion from bus to lorry, as it is believed to be pictured in Slough. The late-David Cantrell Collection

In view of the large numbers of AEC vehicles in the fleet, it is worth digressing a little to talk about the orders that the GWR placed with this London-based company. The AEC company, then based at Walthamstow, had been the first British truck manufacturer to install a moving production line for the building of 'B' type buses for use in London. These buses proved so reliable that the Government acquired a large number of them for the transport of troops in Belgium as well as having a further 10,000 chassis built as 'Y' type lorries for the war effort. After the war the remaining lorries were sold off and the GWR bought a number of these and some new ones.

By comparison the LMS regularly rebuilt and updated their AEC types, but a few of the GWR's lorries saw very long service. In a note accompanying his photographs, the late-David Cantrell wrote. 'In 1949 I received a request from our works at Caerphilly for some parts for a lorry chassis that I didn't know. So I looked into these 'internal-use' lorries, and was amazed to see how old the AECs were. Having been removed from cartage work in Cardiff in the 1930s, they were sent to the works for scrap, but were still at work two decades later.'

Top Left: *Although depicted here in urban surroundings they were equally at home in rural areas and the AECs were chosen to inaugurate the 'Country Lorry Service'.*

Centre Left: *This Y type is carrying a typical load of the time, with goods well packed into very strong packaging to compensate for rough shunting and the number of times they would be transhipped.*

Below: *In their original guise the lorries had only a canvas hood to protect the driver and relied on acetylene lights. Later the vehicles were given a proper cab roof, but retained nearly all of the original fittings, including the solid tyres.*

GROWTH OF THE FLEET.

Above: *A Thornycroft 4-ton PB model dating from 1928.*

By 1920 the fleet had reached 375 vehicles of which about 100 had London as their base, but many of the others were to be found at outlying stations rather than in the populous towns. The reason for this was due to the fact that the majority of the important towns were already well served by horse-drawn services, and these were able to cope with the work as their average journey was less than 3 miles.

The management of the fleet of road vehicles initially came under the auspices of the Superintendent of the Line with certain sections looking after different aspects of the fleet. However this led to an organisation haphazardly evolving, rather than being a department that was specifically planned. This changed in 1922 when the whole of the road staff came together under a Superintendent of Road Transport who exercised control through District Officers in eight areas. The first Superintendent was Mr. F. C. A. Coventry and he remained in the post from 1922 to 1942, having originally been in charge of the road motors from 1902.

Having set up a proper 'Road Motors Department' in London the practice of registering vehicles in such far flung places as Cornwall or Camarthenshire (and the re-registering of vehicles when they moved elsewhere) finally ceased. Henceforward all new vehicles purchased by the GWR were registered in London.

As the motor vehicle fleet grew there was a need for more servicing facilities and many of the larger depots soon received their own maintenance units. Fleet inspection was carried out on a three-monthly basis, and a travelling inspector would submit a report on the man in charge of maintenance at each. Some small parts were kept locally, but the bulk of the stores and parts were kept at Slough and these had to be ordered weekly for despatch by train to the local depot. At this time each driver was allowed one gallon of petrol for every four miles travelled, but a bonus was available if drivers could beat this figure. It was not unknown for benzole to be added to the petrol to eke out the mileage.

19

Above: *Having moved away from the canvas hoods (as seen on page 18), we now show how the GWR offered 'protection' for its drivers with a solid cab roof. However these Burford lorries always looked strange because many had only a half cab due to the fact that the chassis had been downgraded from bus work to lorry work. There was virtually no protection for the driver apart from a small tarpaulin that could be draped over the driver's legs.*

Below: *The GWR also bought a batch of GV battery-electric trucks and these featured the more traditional rear wheel drive, though this time with chains. There was no pretence to driver comforts with the horizontal steering wheel, but we now start to see a slightly fuller cab.* Both Buckinghamshire Railway Society

Reliance was not entirely placed on the internal combustion engine, and the GWR continued experimentation with battery-electric vehicles. Yet, despite their apparent ability to build their own electric vehicles the company looked elsewhere for new ideas and bought seven Orwell and four GV battery-powered trucks. The Orwell trucks must have been tricky to drive and steer since they used front-wheel drive and had two electric motors hung directly on the stub axles. The majority of the Orwell vehicles were based at Paddington, whilst the GV trucks were allocated to Birkenhead.

From about 1922 a new type of vehicle, Fordson tractors, entered service with the GWR and these directly replaced horses on many jobs. It was found that one tractor could easily perform the work of three horses, so the tractor fleet was enlarged and soon included Rushton and International tractors in addition to the Fords. Mention has been made about the agents that worked for the GWR (and other railways), but from the end of World War I these agents began to be taken over and absorbed into the company operation. Occasionally the equipment involved might also be taken over, but as most of this was horse-drawn it was usually not considered as being up to the company's new standards and thus not acquired.

After World War I the growth in bus services was relatively slow, but this situation was influenced by a number of factors, including the availability of new chassis. The supply of ex-WD vehicles helped out, and this position continued up to 1923, when the last batch of war surplus AECs arrived. These vehicles had seen service elsewhere, having been 'loaned' to other railway companies but when they arrived on the GWR they finally saw off the last of the Milnes Daimlers, which by then had seen over 19 years of service. With the demise of the Milnes Daimler vehicles, the fleet was mainly comprised of ex-WD and new AEC chassis, along with models from Burford, Dennis, Gilford, Guy, Maudslay and Thornycroft. Of course the main event of 1922-3 was the reorganisation of Britain's railways into the Grouped companies, but administratively this event had very little effect on the mainly self contained GWR.

However, with changes in the national transport policy, and the Government failing to take up Winston Churchill's proposals for a nationalised public transport system competition began to appear. By 1923 railway bus services got their first real taste of competitive activity, mainly from small independent operators who had purchased small, nimble and fast buses. These competitors could easily outrun the ponderous, but cost-effective AECs, which rumbled along on solid tyres. Accordingly a number of Burford 18-seater buses fitted with pneumatic tyres were obtained to compete with the small independent operators. In 1925 the seeds were sown that would eventually end the bus, coach and tours services operated by the GWR. Throughout the early part of the year solicitors working on behalf of the London and Provincial Omnibus Owners Association, attempted to prove that the GWR did not have the requisite powers to operate bus services. The initial outcome of the discussions that followed, saw the company commencing 'joint operations' on a select number of routes mainly in South Wales, Devon and Cornwall.

Meanwhile the company also took the step towards increasing the fleet size with the purchase of another 35 Burford buses, along with an order for 40 Thornycroft A1 buses. Although the Thornycroft model was a more rugged vehicle than the Burford offering, it was still considered a nimble bus. This order is interesting because the GWR obviously saw that its future remained in providing services in the rural areas rather than in populous towns where they would meet competition from municipal trams and buses. Ironically, to some extent the competition in the country areas could be even more cut-throat than it was in urban areas. In 1926 further orders were placed for Maudslay ML3 and Guy FBB chassis for single-deck bodywork. This particular year also saw the General Strike take place and the GWR bus crews (being members of the NUR) also came out on strike and handed traffic to the competition 'on a plate'!

Towards the end of 1926 a meeting of the various railway companies was held to consider what they should do to protect their bus services in the face of increasing competition from the larger bus companies like National Omnibus, Birmingham & Midland Motor Omnibus (Midland Red), Bristol Tramways and London Transport. The meeting came to the conclusions that; any new services should be designed to feed passengers to the railway, all new services should either be remunerative in themselves or will help to control competition and most importantly as it turned out, will enter into agreement with large companies for co-operative working or to secure a financial interest in such companies. However, just to keep the competition guessing what the GWR was going to do next, orders were placed for a total of 68 new Maudslay chassis. Part of this batch was required to replace the ageing AECs, but the rest were needed for service expansion. For delivery the following year, Thornycroft were asked to supply 20 A2 (4-cyl) chassis for buses and three A6 (6-cyl) chassis for tours work.

Throughout this period the company had also taken over a number of its smaller competitors, and the fleet strength had built up to 206 passenger vehicles made up from the following makes Burford (61), Guy (40), Thornycroft (40), AEC (29), Maudslay (18), Chevrolet (10) and a small number from Daimler, Lancia and Leyland. The latter three makes all originated with companies that had been taken over, but the Chevrolets had been bought new to compete with some of the independent operators.

The progress in the decade after the war was slow but continuous, and by 1928 a grand total of 128 routes had come to be operated by the GWR. The popular view is that many of these routes were entirely concerned in providing rail-feeder services in rural areas! However, it must be remembered that numerous services were commenced in busy towns like Slough, Wolverhampton, Wrexham and Plymouth, with developments also taking place in the Welsh valleys. The GWR also progressively modernised the bus and coach fleet to cope with this growth. In spite of the forward-thinking of the company in up-dating the fleet, in 1928 the Big Four railway companies sought full Parliamentary approval to operate road services for both passengers and goods.

Above: *Although remaining outwardly similar, some of the Y types had their Tylor engine replaced by AEC engines during the 1930s and one or two received pneumatic tyres, though none received modern cabs whilst in GWR ownership. The GWR was adept at exchanging different styles of bodies between vehicles as exemplified here with a dropside and a flat body. The lower photograph shows one of the Y types after its first overhaul where it can now boast a wooden roof over the driver. Neither vehicle is fitted with lights, so one assumes they were not double shifted.*

Below: *Elsewhere in the text we talk about railhead and merchanting services (often in rural areas or provincial town), but this picture is a good example of how the service worked in the inner-city areas. In this case the load is Nestlé powdered baby milk and tins of condensed milk. A book on the Nestlé fleet is one that is being considered for a future volume in this series.*
Both Buckinghamshire Railway Society

Above: *The Associated Daimler Company was a jointly owned marketing company that was meant to combine the best parts of AEC and Daimler engineering. Unfortunately the total was not the sum of the parts and the joint venture did not last long, but the GWR bought some 4/5-ton model 508 trucks. The earliest came with solid tyres, but the later ones had pneumatics from new.*

Below: *A new make of bus, the Morris Commercial (seen below), entered service on the GWR in 1928 with a small fleet being acquired. A solitary ADC chassis was also bodied as a bus, though it must be noted that a further 90 odd ADC goods vehicles also joined the fleet. The final purchasing fling of the GWR, as far as buses was concerned, was to order 52 Maudslay ML3B chassis, 15 Thornycroft BC, 12 Thornycroft A2, 12 Guy OND, and 4 Gilford OT chassis followed by a subsidiary order for 6 small Morris 14-seaters.* The late-David Cantrell Collection

In August 1928 the Railways (Road Transport) Act was passed giving them clear powers to continue to operate road services. This saw the railways begin to purchase shares in bus companies that operated within its defined area. What transpired was that the railway company would transfer certain bus and coach services (along with the vehicles) to an independent bus operator in return for shares in that company. Alternatively the railway would use its new powers to exchange their motor services for half the bus company shares, and in return nominate half the directors. There was a third and vital point, namely the need for the co-ordination of road and rail services. The co-ordination worked well, and in some areas the railways went into partnership with municipal authorities. Indeed, so successful was the joint co-operation, that it led to the complete revision of services in most areas, and some passenger trains were withdrawn and replaced by a bus service in which the railway company concerned had a controlling interest.

The year 1928 saw the introduction of a bus service between two towns (Oxford and Cheltenham) that deserved a direct rail link, but never got one. The buses allocated to this service were the 'luxurious' Thornycroft 15-seaters with roof mounted luggage racks. However the service turned out to be so popular that the small Thornycroft buses had to be replaced by a fleet of Gilford coaches which offered higher seating capacity. At this time the Gilford models were selling well to the independent operators, and the make was renowned both for its fast running with their American petrol engines and for their very competitive pricing. In fact mention of pricing brings to mind the fact that through tickets were available on the bus routes from the major stations. To offer the passengers the best service available, the Gilfords on this route featured heaters, armchair seats, loose cushions and curtains! Apparently the luxury did not stop there, for there was also a vending machine for chocolates, cigarettes and matches.

Then followed a period of change as buses and drivers from both railway companies and bus companies were merged into the 'new' bus companies that had been set up. For instance in conjunction with the old National Omnibus & Transport Company, the operations in various parts of the country became; Western National, Southern National and Eastern National, depending upon which railway company was local to their operating area. Agreements were entered into with various companies including City of Oxford, Thames Valley Traction and Crossville (shared with the LMS). In Wales the GWR bus fleet amalgamated with South Wales Commercial Motors to form Western Welsh.

Other vehicles lost their identity altogether when they joined such companies as Bristol Tramways, Thames Valley, Devon General, and the London General Country Services (which soon became the well-known London Transport). Various vehicles also passed to the Black & White Motorways. By 1934 all of the erstwhile railway-owned bus and coach services had passed to other companies, ending a 31 year pioneering period where the railways had opened up, promoted and developed bus services and left their successors with a well maintained fleet operating a network of well organised routes.

CONTINUOUS IMPROVEMENT

We have emphasised before that throughout the life of the independent Great Western Railway, the company was not afraid to try out new ideas and theories to speed and simplify the handling of goods and parcels traffic. It is interesting to note though that not everyone in management was altogether behind the idea of a railway company running road vehicles. One memorable quote from senior management in the 1930s (referring to a summary of the cartage activities of the Road Transport Department) stated: 'The last ten years coincide with the really useful activities of the Department. Before that date we were busy on the passenger side, but were only allowed to more or less play with the goods service.' In fact the general policy used to be 'Go out and find what the Road Transport Department are doing and tell them not to!'

Above: *An atmospheric shot of the GWR Driver Training School at Taplow, beside the main line in Berkshire. The fleet consisted of two early Scammell Mechanical Horses and a Burford van.*

By 1926 the goods and parcel fleet size had increased to 650 vehicles! This was made up of 343 AEC 'Y Types', 135 Burford 30-cwt vans, 46 Thornycroft 30-cwt vans, 50 Thornycroft 4/5-ton rigids, 21 Ford 1-ton vans, 25 Fordson tractors and a smattering of Commer, Straker Squire, Traffic and Maudslay vehicles. The Maudslay goods vehicles were chassis that had been converted from coaches towards the end of their life, although in one instance a tree fell onto one of the Maudslay coaches rendering an immediate conversion to a livestock-carrying lorry. There was also at least one McCormick Deering 'road converted' tractor that received national press coverage after it pulled a 23-ton load through Birmingham.

Above: *As stated in the text this vehicle was originally a 'cross country bus' operating over the mountain summit at Plynlimmon. It was based on the Morris Commercial D type chassis designed as a 'Subsidy' vehicle that could be called up for military use if needed, as the Government paid the owners of these types of vehicle a 'subsidy' of £120 per year. Both rear axles were driven and there was provision for the fitting of tracks on the bogie. These vehicles were purchased mainly by the Indian Army and could carry 30cwt (1.5-ton) on the road and 1-ton across country. This particular vehicle saw use as a lorry at the end of its passenger carrying days and is seen here near Marlborough.*

Below: *The same vehicle in use with a trailer at the Royal Warwick Show in 1931. The late-David Cantrell also had several pictures of the vehicle in its bus guise, but these were 'borrowed' several years ago by a publishing company who failed to return them. This sad state of affairs is regrettably all too common, and it makes the job of illustrating new books that much harder!*

In 1928 in conjunction with the other Big Four companies the GWR introduced the Road/Rail container which, as its name implies, could be carried on either a rail wagon or road vehicle. The theory behind their introduction was to reduce the amount of double handling and therefore potential for damage or loss whilst giving the customer a door to door service. Now, transferable containers were nothing new (the canals had used them for almost a century), but this time the containers were built to a standard set of dimensions. The container designs consisted of open and closed versions built to two standard sets of floor dimensions and featured a wide variety of individual models that could carry furniture, fish, bicycles, general goods and in the open models items like pipes and bricks. The container service proved to be a real winner and in fact continued in operation until the 1960s when the ISO stackable container was introduced.

With the continuing introduction of new and improved goods services, the railway had to purchase new vehicles to handle them. It is understood that the GWR held shares in at least two motor vehicle manufacturers namely Dennis (Guildford) and Thornycroft (Basingstoke) and it was to these two firms that the GWR often turned. In the very early 1930s a total of 219 new motor vehicles and tractors were ordered at a total cost of £127,000. Of these vehicles Dennis received an order for 108 vehicles of varying sizes. A little later in a further order Thornycroft got a substantial order for 200 chassis, split equally between 30cwt (1.5-ton) and 4-ton models. The Thornycroft Company boasted that this was the largest order ever placed with one manufacturer at that time

The GWR was always ready to publicise any major (or minor) achievement and it often made known several facts about its freight operation. For example, in 1931 it revealed that the London operations handled about 3,300 tons of goods and 34,000 parcels daily, whilst Birmingham's figures were 3,000 tons and 15,700 parcels. A vast and well-organised workforce was necessary to enable this volume of work to be handled and it is worthwhile taking time to explain the way it was done. The goods and parcels were 'trunked' between depots by goods train in closed vans, and on arrival a gang of men with trolleys would rapidly unload the rail vans. These men, directed by checkers and cartage loaders with good local knowledge, would distribute the parcels and packages among the road vehicles, which were generally dedicated to particular districts.

The whole idea behind the collection and delivery operation was for the rail portion of the journey to make the money and for the cartage operation to at least cover its costs. There was a very sound reason behind the competitive charges levied by the railway, in that the low rates charged also meant in theory better utilisation of the rail vans and wagons. If the haulage rates were too high then the traders might be inclined to use their own transport to collect goods from the depots. This might well delay the turn-round of the rail wagons thereby increasing costs. By keeping prices low the railway could almost guarantee that customers would rely on them to deliver the goods.

Despite the cartage operation not setting out to maximise profits, several of the jobs that were accepted by the railway were profitable. For instance there were a number of special cartage jobs, such as the movement of 3,500 tons of steel pipe to Lake Vyrnwy for use on the water pipeline to Liverpool. In another interesting contract crawler tractors found employment hauling 50ft. long steel pipes across country for a new waterworks scheme at Wycombe. All of these contracts came to be offered to the railway companies through their 'Common Carrier' obligation. This obligation to carry any traffic that was offered to them dated from the earliest days of the railways and involved them in maintaining a stock of very specialised road and rail vehicles that saw either occasional or little use. The most obvious example of this was the movement of abnormal loads such as boilers, condensers, turbines and transformers.

One other traffic that deserves a mention was the contract for the removal of felled timber from the Marlborough area. The cut timber was hauled from the forest edge to the station by the only 6-wheeled Morris lorry owned by the company. This vehicle had been purchased to operate a regular tourist bus service as part of a combined road/rail tour over Plynlimmon summit from Devils Bridge to Llanidloes where no real roads existed. The Morris Commercial was a military design and when its passenger carrying days were over its body was removed and the chassis re-bodied and relegated to goods work and special duties at agricultural shows in the summer.

One contract, which to modern eyes seems most unlikely for a railway was the movement of sand and gravel by road tippers, but the GWR was a joint owner of the Theale & Great Western Sand and Ballast Company which operated pits at Theale near Reading. The fleet of vehicles involved on this contract included Foden overtype steam tippers as well as Thornycroft 4 and 6-wheeler tippers. Some of these came to be replaced by Fordson 'B' three-way tippers.

Mention has been made of the tractor fleet operated by the GWR and further description of these vehicles may well be of interest. Most were of Fordson manufacture, but entered service as 'road equipped'. This meant that instead of pneumatic agricultural tyres they came with solid tyres and to ensure grip in inclement conditions, chains were available to fit on the rear tyres. By the late 1920s the ride quality on the solid cobbles of the day, was becoming unacceptable and a number of the vehicles came to be fitted with Muir-Hill internally sprung rear wheels. Another regular addition to the vehicle was a separate drawbar which, when not in use, was carried horizontally above the bonnet. This drawbar was used at times when the tractors had to pull horse drays. By mid-1931 the newer tractors came supplied with pneumatic tyres all round and could boast a GWR-built cab to keep the driver dry. The later versions of the tractor came equipped with trailer brakes.

Just to keep the record straight, during this period the GWR still owned 2,800 horses based at 130 stations. All the food and bedding was distributed from the railway supplies depot at Didcot, a task that involved transporting 6,500 bags of material weekly across the company's network.

Above: *One of the new GWR road-rail containers, on a Serpent C rail wagon.* The late-David Cantrell Collection

Below: *Unusually for the GWR, a batch of Ford 'B' type tippers were bought in 1931 complete with the standard factory cab and what was probably a factory-fitted Anthony Hoists tipper body. They were set to work at Theale moving sand and gravel on behalf of the railway company.*

Above: *One or two of the early AEC Y type 3¹/₂-ton chassis were converted for a trial with demountable bodies. The idea was that a redundant horse dray could stand with a flat-bed platform on top to be loaded whilst the lorry was out delivering with another body. On its return to the depot, the now empty body could be exchanged for a full one. The AECs needed a double acting winch to pull and push the bodies on and off. Whilst certainly forward-thinking, the idea was not to catch on for another 40 years, but then it was a case of what the railways did first, the road haulier did much later.*

Below: *Another demountable system was tried at the South Lambeth depot in London. Here spare lorry bodies were mounted on castors and 'slid' onto a waiting lorry chassis stood in a bay. Again, the system worked satisfactorily, but there was no worthwhile cost or time saving and the development was not pursued.* Both Buckinghamshire Railway Society

When horses were king it was relatively cheap to keep a spare horse or two at the depots and of course there were always spare drays just standing around. This supply of spare drays always enabled the carters to swap empty and full drays at a moment's notice and also gave extra capacity in busy periods. As an interesting aside please note that, the GWR quoted that the cost of the cartage handled at South Lambeth goods depot in 1932 was 5/10d per ton (or about £17.82 at today's values) and employed mainly horse haulage. But by that time there had been a gradual movement from horse to motor traction taking place within the goods service, and this in turn had led to a great deal of concern regarding the supply of spare vehicles.

As the more expensive motors came into operation it was just not feasible to have any spare vehicles above the level required to offer 'cover' when vehicles were off the road for servicing. The Road Department also had to devise ways of keeping these new motors out on the road as long as possible, and cut down the time they spent waiting to be loaded or unloaded in the depots. In their words 'our energies must be directed towards devising demountable machinery which would enable cars (lorries) to get rid of their loads and take on fresh loads with the same expediency as obtained under the regime of the horse'. Consequently, the GWR began experimenting with demountable platform bodies, to speed loading at an early stage.

Three demountable systems came under scrutiny, and these were named 'DCC', 'Turntable' and 'Castor Wheel', and some of these systems are illustrated. One type relied on the 'stand dray' theory; in this a lorry body was slid onto a redundant horse dray and the dray wheeled up to the depot bank for loading whilst the lorry chassis with another body went out on a delivery run. A second system made use of two sets of rollers set longitudinally along the face of the loading bank. Platform bodies from the lorries were slid onto the rollers to be moved to a convenient position to be loaded. The third system is presumed to be similar in operation to one of those mentioned above.

Whilst the systems worked well enough to be taken past the prototype stage it was found that by slight rearrangement of the loading gangs and some pre-planning of the loading process, the demountable systems did not necessarily offer any real advantage or show any savings. The demountable operation at South Lambeth depot using the last mentioned system was mechanically proven, but with as few as two loads per vehicle per day using the system it was easier to employ more loaders. All these experiments were initiated during the second half of the 1920s and some continued into the early-1930s, yet they were soon to be displaced by the 'mechanical horse'. This subject is fully covered in another **Nostalgia Road** book entitled *Mechanical Horses*, but we should perhaps mention the basic fundamentals.

In 1929 the London, Midland and Scottish Railway conducted trials into the ideal means by which to replace the horse and cart on 'Town Cartage' with a mechanical vehicle. Eventually Karrier Motors of Huddersfield agreed to produce a highly manoeuvrable 3-wheeled tractor, which could easily exchange drays, but using petrol power was far more cost effective than a horse.

This vehicle became known as the Karrier Cob, and despite some crudity in the first models, some of the second batch of production models were purchased by the GWR. They entered service initially at South Lambeth goods yard in London where they were matched with horse drays at first, but these drays proved unequal to the task of travelling at speeds of above 4mph, happily shedding wheels and loads with gay abandon. Very soon the railway modified some old Burford chassis to act as trailers for the Cobs and this marked the second stage in articulating part of the GWR cartage operation. Overall the Cob's were not really sturdy enough for railway work and when Scammell Lorries of Watford introduced their Mechanical Horse with a range of dedicated trailers featuring fully automatic coupling they were purchased in large numbers by all the railways.

Further innovations brought in by the railway company included vehicles fitted with 'Moving Floors', a concept initiated by the Principality Wagon Company of Cardiff. The floor was like a large rubber conveyor belt and could be wound forwards or backwards to load or discharge. This concept was usually associated with dustcarts but it also had uses within the railway operation for some bulk loads where it was not possible to tip the vehicle's body as normal.

With the new types of vehicle showing measured success in increased productivity the fleet size continued to increase. By 1936 it had grown to 2,326 lorries, vans and tractors and 1,589 trailers, this figure covering trailers for both horses and lorries to use. Two years later a total of 2,393 vehicles and 1,865 trailers were in service. Growth of the fleet in the last full year before World War II was restricted with few new vehicles being purchased to replace horses. In fact during the war the horse stud increased in number.

One of the GWR's more idiosyncratic ideas was to give each type of non-powered vehicle a name, often with a slightly classical feel to it. The purpose of these names was to reduce the amount of words used in telegraphic communications and was applied to road and rail vehicles. Some examples are noted here:

DYAK A	Scammell 8-ton extendable pole trailer
DYAK F	Scammell 3-ton flat trailer
DYAK G	Scammell 6-ton flat trailer
DYAK OH	Scammell 6-ton fixed side trailer
DYAK OJ	Scammell 6-ton half tilt van trailer
DYAK U	Scammell 3-ton half tilt van trailer
JASON F	Tipping articulated semi trailer
NICO G	Articulated livestock carrier trailer
NUMA D	Twin axled 4-ton drawbar trailer
TITAN D	Heavy-duty low-load drawbar trailer.

Whilst on the subject of trailers, the vast majority of them were fitted with automatic couplings based on the Scammell principle. In the earliest days of the Karrier Cob these vehicles had couplings that were incompatible with the Scammell version, but the later Cobs had Karrier-built Scammell style couplings. There were two sizes of coupling to suit 3- or 6-ton loads and these couplings could be fitted to 3- or 4-wheeled tractors. The variety of trailers was extensive, and trailers were available for almost every conceivable type of job!

Above: This early Karrier Cob Senior is matched to a semi-trailer built up from an early Burford lorry chassis. The trailer features chamfered corners to allow the unit to turn and the coupling is a GWR special that was based on an early American fifth wheel design. Note that the cab did not have the luxury of proper doors, just a canvas screen drawn across the openings. GWR Official

*Below: As detailed in the **Nostalgia Road** book Mechanical Horses it was the Karrier Company of Huddersfield who developed the concept of replacing horses on town cartage by the use of a mechanical tractor for the London Midland & Scottish Railway in 1929-1930. Although the Karrier Cob was never as popular as its cousin from Scammell, the Cob did receive fairly substantial orders from the railway companies including the GWR. This line up of at least 11 tractor units proves the point.*

THE COUNTRY LORRY SERVICE

From the earliest days the theory behind the purchase of mechanically propelled vehicles was that they were not immediately to replace the horse and wagon operations, rather they were to be used to open new services that were beyond the capabilities of the horse. So whilst it may seem strange to find the lorries working in somewhat rural areas, it was these places that were in urgent need of the quality of delivery services that were enjoyed in the towns.

The Country Lorry operation was first started in 1912, when services were introduced between the Welsh towns of Llandyssul and Newquay, and also Haverford West and St. David's. One of the reasons for introducing the service here was that the GWR buses already working in the area were getting overloaded by goods traffic and needed some help. Taking the scheduled bus services as an example these early Country Lorry services also ran to a regular timetable. This new concept gave customers a better service, but it grew very slowly during the period before World War I.

Above: *For once a photograph that hardly needs an explanation. This is a Country Lorry service AEC Y type delivering seed potatoes to a farm near Albrighton, Shropshire.*

After 1918 it grew faster, but it was not until the 1920s that the management altered the concept of operation, from that of a bus service working along specific routes with dedicated services on certain days of the week, into a locally-based collection and delivery service operated as and when required. But once the changes had been made, the GWR could offer services 'as required' to all villages and towns within a certain radius from the railway stations involved. In the 1920s they came up with quite a number of new concepts for the service including the altruistic idea:-

'To help farmers and others whose loads separately might not be enough to justify the individual purchase of motor vehicles, to go where road conditions are too difficult for the ordinary operator, or where the cost of horse-drawn transport is too heavy on account of shoeing expenses'.

Considering that the GWR was meant to be a profit making concern these statements are a joy to behold in these modern self-centred days. To make one further comment on the difficulties faced on these very early services it was stated by the GWR that, 'on one particular run the driver would encounter no less than 17 danger boards within a 16 mile journey'.

These new services gave the farmers and rural businesses a reliable transport service at affordable rates, which were based on the weight of the produce, rather than the value of the goods carried as happened elsewhere on the railway. Country Lorry traffics included animal feed stuffs, fertilisers, seeds, farm implements, agricultural produce and other small consignments of up to 1-ton. There were also available some special reduced rates for traffic in the 2- to 4-ton category, which were put in with a view to encouraging the farmer to use the railway for onward movement of his produce. In 1919 there had been a series of strikes by the railwaymen and on one occasion the strike coincided with harvest time and this forced some of the growers to experiment with road hauliers for the first time. Yet many farmers stayed loyal, and others were won back when it was seen how well the railway's Country Lorry service was working.

By 1928 the GWR were running some 65 Country Lorry services and by the mid-1930s this figure increased to 156 services operating from 115 centres. Further, there really was no effective competition from the road hauliers who would not generally consider this type of work. The road vehicles used most regularly on the service were in the 3- to 4-ton range, as it was not easy for the GWR to operate vehicles of a larger size. It had nothing to do with a lack of traffic since that was hardly ever a problem, but it had more to do with the layout of the goods yards which had been designed in the days of horse-drawn vehicles. This factor imposed a restriction on the length of vehicles to ensure their manoeuvrability between sidings, and this led to the adoption of forward control vehicles wherever possible.

One comment that did not appear in the press releases of the time was the fact that the Country Lorry service also brought about a great improvement in the clearance of rail wagons. Furthermore, farmers no longer had to argue about demurrage claims when they delayed loading of rail wagons since it became the railway's problem. So, whilst seemingly philanthropic, the Country Lorry service brought a major benefit to the railway, in that it could now organise its own collection of traffic. Accordingly railway staff stayed in charge of unloading and loading the wagons, and the sooner they were turned around the sooner they were back in revenue-earning service.

In the days when farmers had done this work, the task at hand was often delayed because Daisy the cow needed milking, or the sheep had got out of the top field, and any one of a million other reasons. Do you remember the scene with the pigs in the Will Hay film *Oh, Mr. Porter*, or John Gregson setting off to market (late) in the comedy *Titfield Thunderbolt*? Such scenes were common in stations up and down the land until the 1960s, but it was a fact of rural life, that the pace of countryside activities did not base themselves on the railway timetable.

Above: *Who says lorry-mounted cranes are a new invention? This photograph was taken at Bewdley in 1929 and it shows an early solution to the problem of materials handling. The Thornycroft driver is demonstrating the ease of loading a heavy taper-sided churn from ground level with a new crane. The station of course has changed considerably over the years, but it still exists to serve passengers on the Severn Valley Railway.*

Below: *The AEC 'Y' types were ponderous looking beasts, yet were an essential component of the GWR road vehicle operation. This particular AEC advertises the Country Lorry Service on the enamelled plate on the cab side. This vehicle had originally been used for passenger carrying with a Charabanc body and was converted to goods carrying on receipt on newer and more suitable bus chassis.*

Above: *An essential part of farming was the movement of livestock. The railway companies could move anything from a single pig to complete farms. In 1936 the GWR chose this impressive Ford Model 51 and converted it to a 6-wheel truck to work as a livestock carrier. The modern image of the Ford bonnet assembly was in complete contrast to the rather basic cab structure.*
Buckinghamshire Railway Society

Below: *The long distance movement of milk from farm to dairy was a business built up and encouraged by the railway companies. In this instance an ADC 508 truck from 1929 is collecting a mixture of full (or delivering empty) taper-sided and parallel sided churns in the Shrivenham area.*

The company was at pains to point out that during the late-1920s and early-1930s an increase of 30% in traffic handled proved that the railways were able to listen to the customers and obtain new revenue. Some statistics from 1936 might be of interest to the reader in that the company operated some 1,968 petrol vehicles, plus a small number of steam and heavy oil lorries. The principal makes in the fleet were Thornycroft (877), AEC (318), Scammell (205), Morris Commercial (176), Ford (132), Dennis (111), Karrier (30). There were 806 trailers designated for use with these motor vehicles. The tractor fleet numbered 59, mainly of Fordson, Latil and Leyland manufacture.

Following the innovations of the Barham family, who established the Express Dairy Country Milk Supply Company, the movement of milk from the country to the towns and cities rapidly became an important source of traffic for the railway. The railway involvement in the movement of fresh, clean milk to the industrialised areas involved both the local collection of churns and its onward movement by express passenger train. The railways also had a lot to do with the change from the old fashioned tapered-sided churn to the parallel-sided churn after World War I, during which time it had been found that the women porters employed on the work could not easily move churns by themselves. There was another reason behind the change, as more straight sided churns would better fit onto a lorry platform therefore increasing the volume of milk carried on each vehicle.

After the Grouping the railways also worked closely with the milk supply companies in the development of dairies and creameries alongside railway lines, where milk could be taken by Country Lorry services and processed. It would then be sent on by rail in glass-lined tank wagons, but this is really another story. The dairies often had 'egg-packing stations' and these were also served by the same lorries. Unlike the general Country Lorry service in the mid-1930s the milk collection rounds did operate to a fairly strict timetable!

In addition to the regular Country Lorry services, there was a large number of other services which today would seem impractical for the railways to carry out. Yet before World War II, it was commonplace for the railway companies to move cattle and sheep between markets, whilst sugar beet was a regular traffic during its season. Hay and straw would utilise vehicles fitted with hay ladders. As the country roads began to improve and 'metalled' surfaces were provided, the railways would carry large quantities of tar in rail tankers to stations, where it would be decanted into drums and delivered within a radius of ten miles. The Country Lorry fleet would also be used to take wooden telegraph poles to various locations for erection by GPO engineers. There was even a 'throughout by road' service for the delivery of films between cinemas and the film distribution companies. One other well known service was rendered to the promoters of county agricultural shows, for whom the GWR would undertake the movement of stands, exhibits, exhibitors and animals between shows during the summer. With English summers often being wet, the most important piece of equipment on this service was a Fordson caterpillar tractor, which was regularly used to extricate other vehicles and equipment from the mud and mire.

We have mentioned that the Country Lorry services handled items like fertilisers, seed and so on but we must add that manufacturing companies were also given a complete transport, warehousing and distribution service by the GWR. The idea behind what was called the Railhead Service, was to introduce more freight onto the rails and then offer a number of add-on services that the road hauliers could not possibly attempt to compete with.

From these small beginnings sprang a major distribution network that would now be described as logistics, and like many other ideas that today are thought of as being new or 'state of the art', they were often devised by the railways. Railhead Services gave manufacturers the ability to transport their goods in bulk by rail at low rates, to a railway owned warehouse where railway staff would pick orders and arrange for the delivery of the orders to the retailer the next day or on any specified day. Such services first began in March 1927.

There were in fact three slightly different Railhead schemes; one gave an exclusive contract for individual firms whereby 2-ton GWR vans were employed on the distribution of that particular company's commodities. In fact the GWR got so involved that they would also collect empties, issue credit notes and even unpack the goods and put them on display if requested. Needless to say none of these extra services came free, yet the operation remained successful since the overall cost was well below what it would cost a manufacturer to set up their own 'stand alone' service.

Where any one vehicle was not continuously employed for a single manufacturer, say working just a few days a week on their work, the GWR would have removable boards stating the name of the customer mounted on the van sides. However, if the van was fully committed to one manufacturer then the van could be painted in that customers' livery and the drivers wore that firm's uniform.

The second of the Railhead schemes gave smaller customers the ability to get goods delivered within a 20 to 30 mile radius of the main depot at a flat rate per ton. This was a much simpler system than the normal complex rates that the railway charged according to distance, value of goods and a host of other factors. Indeed these factors were so difficult to comprehend, that some people joked that even the phases of the moon had some influence on the rates charged. This flat rate was also extended in the third scheme to railhead distribution by the Country Lorry service, but would only apply in a fairly restricted number of cases.

This type of contract where the transport operator took over the whole distribution operation from the manufacturer was the beginning of the contract hire business that is so prevalent now. Today contract hire is the mainstream business of companies like Wincanton, Hays and Ryder, yet it was the GWR that first had the idea! It was later carried on by British Railways, then National Carriers and currently by the National Freight Company under the EXEL banner all acting as legitimate successors to the Great Western Railway. The railhead services saw rapid growth and soon became well-established in centres like Birmingham, Swansea, Cardiff, Exeter and Bristol all covering an area within a 20-30 mile radius.

Above: *The GWR had a long standing relationship with the Cadbury company and this 1931 Morris Commercial TX type 30cwt (1.5-ton) van was one of many on contract to the chocolate company. This was one of the last Morris Commercial models to feature the cast radiators, very soon the company commenced using pressed metal radiator surrounds, as seen below.*

Below: *The Morris chassis was a popular choice for the vehicles that the GWR were operating on the Contract Hire service. In this case a C type dating from 1936 is seen in 1939 with a special body built to the specification of Macfarlane Lang, complete with roof rack for empty biscuit tins. It will be noted that the vehicle carries the 'Royal Warrant', and it is an interesting aside that we know of at least 30 of the firms who used the GWR Contract Hire service had their vans liveried with the words....by appointment to....!*
Both Buckinghamshire Railway Society

Above:
A further Morris Commercial TX type employed in the contract hire service, this time for Hughes Biscuits. It is painted in this firm's livery and sign-written accordingly. However its GWR ownership can be identified by the small white plate on the vans side below the roof-line and just above the capital 'H' in the name Hughes. The vehicle carries a mixture of electric and acetylene lighting and a roof rack for carrying empty tins.

Below: *Where a contract hire customer did not want a full time vehicle, the GWR would often supply vehicles with removable name plates. In this instance though the GWR livery has been retained along with the addition of the user's name. Again a Morris Commercial C type is in use.*
Both Buckinghamshire Railway Society

Famous household names that used the railhead and warehousing services included McVities, Cadburys, Lever Bros., The Cement Marketing Company and Rowntrees. It was very cheering to recall that during the 1930s the GWR were regularly asked to increase its levels of service by their customers in response to increased demand by the ultimate customer.

By the 1930s the practicable cartage distance had been significantly increased by the introduction of motor vehicles in place of horses, and this led to the possibility of reducing the number of goods depots whilst still retaining or even bettering the level of service required by the customer. This scheme was called 'Traffic Concentration' or zonal schemes for short and about 20 such schemes came to be operated by the early-1930s, with further additions in the planning stages when war preparations began to assume greater importance.

After the war this scheme was updated and later became an essential part of the BR Modernisation Scheme, which saw its application in all of the British Railway regions in the 1950s. The theory behind Zoning was to allow overnight delivery of small consignments (i.e. less than wagon load traffic) between any two stations. With the handling of this traffic concentrated at a smaller number of depots, it was possible to make up full rail wagon loads between depots. When this was combined with greater use of road transport the overall level of delivery service improved.

Throughout this text we have endeavoured to keep to the maxim that simplicity is best and have not gone into any great detail of the individual models of vehicles used by the GWR. The reason is partly lack of space and partly that many of the readers of this book may not be interested. However, that does not preclude us from introducing certain details such as the Standard Cab, which the GWR decided to introduce.

Throughout the period covered by this book, the GWR's Swindon works was capable of building bodies for the vehicles it used, whether they were buses or lorries. Generally speaking the vehicles bought up to the mid-1930s arrived with a cab supplied by the manufacturer, but many of these cabs were not thought to be up to the standard required by the company. Accordingly the GWR designed a universal cab design that could fit all current makes of vehicle in the late-1930s. This cab boasted a sliding door on the driver's side, which enabled him to lean out of the cab and be able to reverse safely. In addition the cab was built to the extreme width of the vehicle which enabled the driver to see 'round ' the van body.

The only problem with this idea was often the manufacturer's positioning of the handbrake, as this could make it difficult for the driver to enter and leave the cab easily. The first instance of a GWR cab being fitted to a chassis was with a Fordson 7V. Thereafter it was then found on a variety of vehicles during the war, but is probably best known on the Thornycroft 'Nippy' chassis both in rigid and articulated tractor form. The cab was supplied right up to 1948 and some of them came to be built by outside contractors such as Hampshire Car Bodies.

LEGAL POWERS

In 1914 an article appeared in the *Commercial Motor* asking 'have the railways a right to the road?' complaining about railway companies asking specifically for road powers (a portent of things to come perhaps). In fact back in 1902 the GWR's solicitor had expressed some misgivings as to whether the railway had the right to operate road services and in 1904 had included clauses in a Parliamentary railway bill that should have ensured their right to operate all sorts of road services. With the gradual introduction of new cartage services that came to be operated by mechanical vehicles, which were able to offer more comprehensive services than were ever envisaged under the railway's original acts of Parliament, various concerns came to be voiced over the legality of the operation of road services. The Railways Act of 1921 made the situation a little less confused and seemed to legalise road movement of goods.

From the passing of an Act of Parliament in 1928 the railways were definitely allowed to carry 'goods throughout' by road, and they were no longer obligated to undertake part of the journey by rail. What this meant for the railways was that they could now legitimately move goods directly between supplier and customer by road, an option not legally open to them before 1928.

Above: *This is an early post-war Foden DG winch equipped tractor fitted with a Gardner 5LW engine. The drawbar low load trailer is a Priestman diesel face shovel.* National Railway Museum

This in turn meant that certain traffics could be given a much faster service with less intermediate transhipping and therefore less potential of damage. It also led indirectly to the closure of some of the smaller goods depots where it became more practicable to trunk the goods from a larger depot. On a more local basis this allowed the distribution of a trader's goods from his warehouse to customers in the same town or indeed from shop to residence.

The introduction of the 1930 Road Traffic Act brought in a number of standards relating to the construction and use of road vehicles as well as the need for third party insurance. From this date the maximum gross weight for a 4-wheel truck became 12-tons and 19-tons for 6-wheelers. It also spelt the end for many of the heavier steam lorries and waggons by introducing licensing fees based on unladen weight. This also had the immediate effect of bringing about a rapid increase in the use of pneumatic tyres instead of solid ones. There was also a restriction placed on the number of hours that a driver could remain on duty or driving, but this particular part of the regulations seemed to be regularly ignored by the road hauliers.

Top Left: *This 1945 3-ton Mechanical horse has what looks like a Swindon-built cab, complete with a real drivers door, but note that even at this late date these vehicles still had to be wound up to start.*

Centre Left: *The GWR designed the 'Safety Cab' to fit all makes of chassis and two versions are shown in this picture and that following. Both vehicles are Thornycroft Nippy tractor units fitted with Scammell 6-ton automatic couplings, but this is a 1939 model.*

Bottom Left: *This is the post-war version (c1947), and whilst very similar to the pre-war version a close study of the pictures will reveal noticeable differences.* All GWR Official

The railway vehicles were taxed in the same manner as haulage vehicles and the tax rates ranged from £15 per year for a 1-tonner to £60 per year for a 5-tonner, that would be about £900 and £3,600 respectively at today's prices. In fact at the beginning of 1932 the company had to pay out £59,000 in taxation fees for some 1,500 vehicles, today that sum would just about tax 15 gross weight vehicles but in real terms would cost around £3 million! Another anomaly to today's attitudes to profit is that the railway road fleet was never meant to make any money.

Following on from the effects of the industrial depression, with the cut-throat pricing practices used by the road hauliers, the railway companies had come to the conclusion that the road powers granted to them earlier were not in themselves sufficiently strong to enable them to meet road transport competition. As a result they made strong representations for the institution of some measure of control of road haulage. On more than one occasion the GWR made it known that their energies were spent more on fighting road competition than giving management time to upgrade their services to industry. As a result of some fairly strong lobbying, a committee under Sir Arthur Salter was set up by Parliament in 1932. Its remit was to consider the incidence of highway costs in relation to the contributions made by the various types of mechanically propelled vehicle, as well as considering what economic measures might assist both branches of the transport industry to perform under equitable conditions. This in turn led to the Road Traffic Act 1933 which, amongst many other points, stated that all commercial vehicles would need a licence to continue operating. Three main types of licence were involved:

The A licence was needed for general haulage;
The B licence was a very restricted form of licence for specific goods or for operating within a restricted radius.
The C licence enabled manufacturers to carry only their own goods, but take them anywhere with no restrictions.

To increase the number of A or B licences owned by any one haulier, the applicants had to prove a need for the service or prove that the needs were not adequately met by either an existing haulier or the railway companies. Just to make things more difficult competitors were able to object to the issue of additional licences by the Traffic Commissioners.

Although the railways were automatically granted licences for the payload tonnage of existing vehicles they had to pay for the privilege! In August 1933 (90 years after Pickfords first began cartage operations for the GWR) the Big Four railway companies jointly gained control of two of the country's largest road hauliers by purchasing the shares of Pickfords and Carter Paterson. Pickfords were a general carriers operating a road-based delivery network, but they did have some rail trunking of traffic. They had been acquired by Hays Wharf in 1920 and expanded into many new areas of transport. In 1932 Pickfords commenced their London Suburban Goods Service which was in direct competition with the already established Home Counties Express service operated by their great rivals Carter Paterson who were based in London and Manchester and acted in direct competition with the railway parcel services.

The railways' take-over of these two concerns was by far more to do with the addition of services to those offered by the 'Big Four' rather than a straight amalgamation, so the networks worked side by side. One big change came as Pickfords began to utilise railway-owned land for some new depots. By 1943 the Carter Paterson business was in the process of being transferred into the control of Hays Wharf to make just one road based parcels carrier.

During the 1920s and 1930s competition between road carriers could almost be described as cut-throat with numerous firms touting for business, including such well known names as McNamara, Beans Express, Suttons and Globe Express. Their natural target was the railways, where delays in reconstruction and under-funding had prevented a return to the highly efficient services of pre-World War I.

Top Right: *This is a 1932 Thornycroft featuring a 'moving floor' built by the Principality Wagon Company in Cardiff. The floor could be hand wound backwards or forwards for loading or unloading and was designed as an alternative to a tipper body where the body could not be tipped due to height or stability problems. Quite a number of these lorries were used by the Chief Civil Engineer's Department (including this one), and thus do not really form part of our description of what were 'revenue-earning' vehicles. Even so, the subject of engineering department vehicles can not be lightly ignored, even if such pieces of railway-owned equipment were not widely photographed. The subject is therefore open for another* **Nostalgia Road** *book, and we would appeal to readers for help.*

Centre Right: *The Nippy was a 3-ton rigid, magically converted to carry six tons by virtue of the coupling and uprated brakes along with different carburettor jets! Here is the Thornycroft Nippy in 3-ton drop-side form complete with GWR safety cab.*

Bottom Right: *The Ford Model 51 appeared in a variety of guises including this 1936 drop-side bodied 6-wheeler. The grey livery denotes departmental use, once again note the hand written number on the cab side, presumably the original owner of the photograph wanted to keep his fleet list up to date!*

The campaign was successful, and nimbler road hauliers were able to erode substantial chunks of the railway's most profitable business. Unfettered by such restrictive legislation as the need to publish rates and the common carrier concept whereby the railways had to accept any traffic that they came to be offered, road haulage could pick and choose its traffics. This seriously hurt the 'Big Four' companies, and from 1938 they campaigned for a 'square deal' to enable them to compete head on with the road hauliers.

What the railway campaign wanted was the freedom from pricing and product constraints, that is to obtain an economic price for each service or abandon that service and the goods handling facilities that went with it. The official reply to the campaign eventually came from the Transport Advisory Council on 19th May 1939. The Council 'agreed that the classification of merchandise and fixing of standard charges should be repealed', yet made no recommendation regarding the publication of rates. A number of other points were aired, but really nothing changed because the campaigning by the combined railway companies was dramatically and effectively ended by the onset of World War II. This, in turn, made road/rail co-ordination essential and in fact led directly to the transport nationalisation plans of the post war era. Indeed, we can reveal that the Government stalled the answer to the railway's wish to get their 'Square Deal' to ensure that all facilities remained intact prior to the war, ostensibly in the needs of 'national interest'.

Given the overall state of the road haulage industry at the start of the conflict, it is very lucky that the railways retained such a large infrastructure because, as Winston Churchill stated, 'Without them we would not have survived the war.' Once the war had ended the Government published plans in the 1947 Transport Act which appeared to give the railways just the gift that they needed, apparent control over the long distance road haulage operators and no more competition! Unfortunately as they say 'the best laid plans of mice and men', and the one type of haulier not involved in nationalisation, the 'own account' operator, really came into his own, but that's another story.

Top Left: *A 1932 Morris Commercial Courier 5-ton lorry fitted with a double deck milk churn body for use on a Nestlé contract based at Lostwithiel, Cornwall. The chassis design was based on the Dictator bus.*

Centre Left: *In North London some parcels services were jointly operated between the GWR, LNER and Metropolitan lines as part of the contract forged when the Great Central opened its new main line into London. The vehicle shown here was a 2/3-ton Thornycroft.*

Bottom Left: *Although the 1-ton Morris Commercial vans looked reasonably modern from the side views, from the front they looked positively archaic. It is interesting to see that the sign-writing on this one has been modified to allow an advertisement board to be fitted on the van side. Note that the vehicle only has sidelights!*

RAILHEAD DETAILS.

The growth in fleet size continued during the mid- to late-1930s, and we can give a brief outline of the type of operations in part of South Wales as an example of the situation.

At Newport in Monmouthshire in 1939 the parcels service had exclusive use of seven road vans based at the station and dealt with approximately 5,000 parcels daily split roughly 50/50 between items received and forwarded. In addition to this there was a considerable volume of transfer traffic in connection with the Welsh valley stations. The goods traffic was dealt with at the High Street station.

At High Street the goods shed could house 47 rail wagons under cover with a further 100 handled outside. There existed 80 berths for road vehicles, although a total cartage fleet of 97 vehicles worked from the goods shed. Surprisingly the motor lorries only numbered 18 with the balance made up of horse-drawn vehicles. However, when it is considered that the delivery area of the depot was with a maximum 2 1/2 mile radius the preponderance of horse-drawn units makes sense. Within the town of Newport there existed three other rail fed depots:

Above: *A typical railhead photograph is seen here at Cardiff where the vehicles in view are mainly Thornycrofts.*

Dock Street Depot (mainly agricultural goods like grain, oilcake, potatoes and fertilisers); Mill Street Depot (mainly full rail wagon loads and coal); Liswerry Depot (mainly coal).

To complete the picture of how important the railway network was to an important manufacturing town like Newport, there were a total of 33 private sidings connected to factories. In addition the docks exported huge quantities of Welsh coal as well as handling imported iron and bauxite ore, timber and raw sugar, all of which came to be forwarded by rail.

We might next look at Cardiff (pictured above) in 1939 some 13 years after the initial railhead service commenced. By this date the dedicated fleet numbered up to 25 motor vehicles and served an area up to 30 miles from the base. Within Cardiff depot the road fleet numbered 263 vehicles of which only 51 were motor lorries, yet the general merchandise traffic totalled (in 1938) 990,438 tons inwards and 1,132,473 tons forwarded. In addition to this was a total of about 7 million tons of coal.

THE LAST DECADE

Bearing in mind that the GWR had been formed back in 1835, the year 1935 was to mark a special point in British Railway history. A centenary of spectacular achievement was recorded in a special supplement to *The Times* newspaper that year (later re-printed in book form), and covered all aspects of the company's history. In all that had to be discussed, there was not much room to talk about the road services, but nevertheless several pages were dedicated to the subject. Much of it covered ground already discussed in this book, but it concluded with a statement that is relevant to the GWR's view of the future for the road service after 1935.

'A stage has been reached at which, apart from the capital represented by Great Western cartage equipment, the company's financial interests in road transport are so extensive as to exceed in amount the share capital authorised by their Act of Incorporation. The policy from which this position has resulted has also involved the emphasis upon the complementary rather than the competitive relationship of the two forms of transport, and in this spirit it may be confidently anticipated that "the best is yet to come".'

That 'the best was yet to come', was a strong promise indeed, but the 1930s were a real time of change for the Big Four companies. This was reflected in the social situation of the British people, as factories were idle and around 3,000,000 people (a quarter of the British workforce) were on the dole in 1932-3. In 1934 the 'out of work' figure had dropped to 2,000,000 and a process of change began to take place. Much of the work was generated by a series of Government-led financial initiatives, some of which were directed to help re-build the railways but were mostly concerned with re-armament or defensive measures.

The demand for steel began to increase dramatically, especially in South Wales where new facilities were provided, and in the three years from 1933 output climbed by a staggering 80%. Coal traffic, again a staple business for the GWR in Wales, increased to a national 240,000,000 tons in 1937. Passenger figures on the GWR had increased by 20% and express parcels had grown by a massive 182% on 1929. Even so almost all of these figures were well down on pre-1914 figures, with the exception of the express cartage service, which was being used more and more by industry who were seeking to reduce overall delivery times.

Top Left: *This 1939 Thornycroft/Scammell articulated is displaying one of its less redeeming features, the miniature sliding door on the passenger side. Later designs of the Safety cab had a more accessible hinged door. The trailer is a Scammell 6-ton drop frame, which had a wide variety of uses including departmental use in both the civil engineering and mechanical engineering departments. In all some 15 were allocated to Swindon Works.*

Top Right: *In contrast with the previous photograph the driver of this Thornycroft Nippy rigid lorry had quite a commodious entry to the cab. To make way for the sliding door the body was cut away on the offside. Even as late as 1947 these vehicles still boasted a starting handle.*

Centre Right: *A much earlier Thornycroft was this 1929 six-wheel PB model. Fitted with double dropside it would have been utilised for the delivery of full wagon-load traffic direct from the goods yards to the customer.*

Bottom Right: *These quaint beasts are two 1933 Thornycroft Handy 2-tonners and they are seen making use of old railway wagon tarpaulins to act as a tilt cover to protect the parcels that are being loaded. They are part of a batch of 50 of these vehicles purchased in the early-1930s.*

The critical years from 1914 to 1934 had shown one thing however, that both industry and the public wanted faster and more efficient service, and that the old 'slow but sure' pipeline method of supply was no longer commercially acceptable. The railways were starting to adapt to this type of demand, and as new equipment was brought in, the acquisitions were designed to reflect these changing circumstances. The increase in express-rated goods stock is a specific indication of the new services, as is the development of container services that could offer a factory to end-user service without the need for any handling of the goods en-route.

During the decade after 1929, the GWR expended no less than £13,000,000 on capital projects. The Treasury through the Railways (Agreement) Act, enabled Government-approved schemes to attract loans at very advantageous interest rates, providing the GWR with substantial chunks of money. As the Government was more interested in improving locomotive handling, strategic track improvements and goods facilities, it is little wonder that passenger services did not see the same level of investment as the other three areas of operation. With respect to goods service improvements, certain shortfalls in road delivery and collection services had identified these as being a 'weak link' in the system during World War I, so improvements were authorised. Of these improvements, the development of the Zonal scheme, was the most logical step forward. It also has to be said that the mechanisation of the cartage fleet, predominantly developed on the aforementioned LMS strategy, was an indirect result of the same official demand for improvement.

Above: The Fordson 7V chassis was a relatively rare vehicle in railway ownership. The LNER and GWR operated a few and the LMS were allocated some during World War II, but it was not a very popular model. This particular truck No.A3014 (FLL 388) was new in 1938 and was fitted with a Swindon-built safety cab, but when this is added to the standard Ford scuttle it makes a rather grotesque combination. For a while this lorry was allocated to the rural services operation in the Wolverhampton district.

Below: The safety cab and Fordson combination actually seemed a lot better in van form, with the metal scuttle looking less obvious. This particular van, No.A3082 (FYU 207) was destined for use as a Civil Defence control vehicle during World War II. Government funding was given for several railway road vehicles, on the proviso that they had a dual role. Both Buckinghamshire Railway Society

By 1935 the worst effects of World War I, the General Strike, and the Depression were starting to be overcome. Although it was a slow process, change was evident in every corner of the British railway network. The Southern had progressed well into its electrification programme, the LMS had begun to clear up its atrocious accident rate, whilst generally accelerating main line services, and the LNER had introduced its streamlined trains and also set their sights on a world speed record for a steam locomotive.

The GWR had accomplished a whole host of 'firsts', but it was in their safety record and the introduction of Automatic Train Control that did so much to set them apart from everyone else. In confident mood then, and with around 100 years of experience behind them, the GWR could make its promises for the future, but dark clouds loomed on the horizon. By 1936 the level of investment in railway development was clearly being directed to those schemes that would show a 'national advantage', and from 1937 onwards primary investment went into breakdown, heavy lifting and repair equipment. The following year the theme changed to Air Raid Precaution and anti-gas training.

As had been the case in 1914, the railways were again taken under Government control when war broke out in September 1939. Once again it fell to the Railway Executive Committee, a group of senior railway managers designated by the Government, to ensure that traffic on the railways was prioritised according to national need. They also had the responsibility of turning over railway property for military use, and the allocation of manufacturing capacity within the railway workshops for 'war work'. An immediate effect on the railway road fleet was to see a transfer of vehicle body-building capacity to military vehicle work. A variety of bodies were built for the Army and Royal Air Force, with smaller numbers being produced for the Royal Navy. The GWR works also did conversions on AEC, Bedford and Commer-Karrier chassis to form searchlight platforms, anti-aircraft gun platforms, airfield rapid response defence units, barrage balloon winch wagons, gas decontamination vans and a whole array of other vehicles concerned with Air Raid Precautions.

Existing stock was also taken over for military use, especially the newer low-load and heavy haulage tractors, and in addition to the 79 locomotives taken over by the Government, at least 115 road vehicles were requisitioned. A number of GWR vehicles, whilst remaining in company ownership, were also converted or adapted for ARP use. Several Thornycroft 2-ton express parcel vans were converted to fire engines, and given Merryweather trailer pumps. At the same time at least 36 Morris Commercial vans were turned into emergency ambulances.

All these vehicles retained the GWR livery and many still carried advertising on the side, but one wonders how people would react today if they saw an ambulance advertising the glories of Devon, or a fire engine promoting Sudso soap. Some of these ARP vehicles were allocated 'full-time' to their new duties, but most were 'operational as normal' during the day, converting to their 'wartime' role as night-time (and the threat of bombing) came on.

The evacuation of children (and other 'at risk' groups) from the major cities imposed a heavy work load on the railways all through the war years, as large numbers of people were moved from the cities to rural areas. The GWR bus services provided a link between the stations and the 'billeting areas', but the traffic was not solely confined to the two major evacuation programmes of Autumn 1939 and the Spring of 1940. All through the war evacuees would return home when the threat of danger subsided, only to return to the country when the bombs started falling again, in addition visits by relatives to those billeted away from home kept up the pressure.

New traffic flows in food were handled by the railways, and one example was the Walls Ice Cream factory at Acton, where all production on confectionery ceased and fruit juice, powdered milk, powdered egg and tinned sausage took over. Thousands of bangers left the Acton factory each week, so the GWR moved five extra mechanical horses and 12 semi-trailers to the local goods yard to cope with the traffic. Another new traffic was in gas masks, which the GWR distributed over large areas, and in all created 152,312 journeys throughout the system.

The railways also had to cope with a severe loss of staff due to the call up for men to enter the armed forces. This loss was to some extent overcome by the employment of women as cartage staff and drivers as well as the retention of staff who were due for retirement, but there were still requests for existing staff members to recruit friends and family to relieve the situation. Even where staff remained in their post-war occupations, the scene of things had changed. Everybody and everything was expected to work harder and, when the day's work was done, they then took on other duties as well. These duties ranged from service as ARP Wardens, to being members of the Home Guard or the Auxiliary Fire Service, whilst others were attached to the ambulance service. Many carmen became Special Constables and were allocated patrols of railway depots and warehouses in order to reduce the amount of pilferage and 'black market theft' activity.

As we have mentioned, railway road vehicles also undertook dual duty, and many cartage vehicles were seconded to 'emergency repair works'. After their day's service was done, the vehicles would roll out of the city centres to strategic points in the suburbs. Here emergency repair depots, along with substantial stores of track and building repair materials, were established in order to repair the infrastructure and get trains moving should the railways suffer bomb damage. Naturally, in case of the severance of rail communication, road vehicles were imperative to get men and materials to the repair site and thus pave the way for engineers' trains to start running. Even so, not all road vehicles were taken out of the city's on a night, and the GWR lost around 200 road vehicles due to bomb damage. These losses were relatively light, especially in view of the fact the GWR suffered no less than 1,202 bombing incidents, ranging from the tiny station at Newton Abbot to the main goods yards around London. The worst loss was seen during the bombing of Birmingham on 24th-25th October 1940, when no less than 24 horse drays and three motor vehicles were lost in one single incident.

Above: *The Thornycroft Company produced the Trusty design before the war and the GWR bought some and fitted them with yet another version of the Safety Cab. This time the drivers sliding door is quite small due to the positioning of the front axle. They must have been quite difficult to get into and out of during a full days collection and delivery work.*

Below: *Although the Dennis make was not unknown to the GWR, but it was not a common type in their later fleets. However, the shortage of vehicles (due to a Government-led export drive) after World War II meant that most road transport concerns had to make do with what was available. In this instance a Dennis Jubilant 6-wheeler was purchased to carry heavier loads and replace an older Thornycroft 6-wheeler. Another view of this vehicle (HGP 734 - Fleet No S9012) shows that its tailgate was painted entirely in cream, and it also had a slot that allowed the rear lights to show through when the tailgate was dropped.* R. N. Hannay

Above: The Morris Commercial T type vans had a second life during the war, and several were converted to auxiliary fire tenders to make up the shortages in conventional fire appliances. Complete with ladder and towed fire pump trailer they gave quick response to incendiary devices falling on railway property.

Below: The Morris company supplied a large number of vehicles to the GWR including a fleet of 'C' type semi forward control 2-ton chassis. These vehicles came complete with a factory-built cab, but Swindon supplied the body. In this case two GWR aumbulancemen are seen in a 1939 ARP 'publicity' picture demonstrating their gas masks whilst working with a 1934 model express parcels van converted for use as an emergency ambulance. These vehicles did their normal day's work with their stretchers fastened back to the sides of the van. Both the late-David Cantrell Collection

In connection with bomb damage, a number of GWR cartage vehicles were allocated to permanent duties with the 'Emergency Housing Repair Scheme'. Every morning (starting at about 5am), the carmen would begin delivering supplies of brick, timber, slates, glass and plywood to the areas that had been blitzed during the night. A GWR 6-ton mechanical horse was converted into a rigid vehicle to form a cement mixer, and it worked with two other mechanical horses that carried trailer loads of sand and cement to the repair sites.

One of the most amazing logistical exercises ever undertaken by any company up to the early part of the war involved the distribution of air raid shelters. The operation involved nearly everyone who worked for the road cartage service within any of the big four railway companies. These shelters were an assembly of flat and curved corrugated iron sheets placed in peoples gardens to offer some protection in bombing raids. An initial order for 180,000 tons of steel sheets, channels and accessories had been placed by the Government to make 400,000 shelters to house up to four or five people.

The problem in logistics was caused by the fact that 19 different firms made the steel sheets, 38 more made the angles, tees and channels whilst a further 21 made the nuts and bolts. Two thirds of the sheets were manufactured in South Wales, with most of the fixings made in the West Midlands, all of which had to be moved by the GWR. Each shelter consisted of 21 parts including a bag of accessories, and any one shelter would consist of parts made by five firms. All of these parts had to arrive at the destination depot in the right order on the correct day to enable local delivery to be affected.

When it is considered that the GWR alone was forwarding over 1,000 rail wagon loads of sheets weekly it can be envisaged what a major headache it was for the operators. Of course the problems did not end at the railhead, for the GWR road fleet then took over. The drivers or carmen had to deliver all the parts and components to the exact position in each householder's garden even if this meant going through the house. In doing this work, the men had to be very careful not to knock over any ornaments or dislodge pictures off the walls.

Yet despite these extra duties and dangers, the work of the railways had to go on. However, as far as London and the major cities were concerned, a lot of the work had to be concentrated into daylight hours, as the threat of bombing (and black-out precautions) imposed severe restrictions on night-time operations. Even so the levels of freight traffic increased dramatically in the first half of the war, and in 1942 the GWR ran no less than 725,000,000 loaded wagon miles. This was an increase of 30% over the 1939 total, but it grew even higher between 1942 and 1944. Much of this traffic involved collection and delivery work by the road vehicle fleet, and in some places large numbers of railway lorries were moved to a new depot to cope with the demand. Near Pencoed in Wales a new munitions factory, built into the side of a hill, took no less than three years to construct. All the material was brought to Bridgend or Pencoed goods depots and then moved by road, all 145,000 tons of it! The movement of 12,000,000 bricks occupied a fleet of no less than eight mechanical horses and 27 trailers working flat out for over two years.

This was not an isolated instance and all over the system the GWR's road vehicles were being used to their maximum capacity, and overall the fleet's productivity rose by 20%. With the continuing shortage of petrol, oil and rubber throughout the war it fell upon the lot of the trusty carter and his horse to handle even more goods than usual on his (or her) rounds. The Government made available small numbers of new vehicles to the railways, but it was really a case of make do and mend rather than replace with the majority of commercial vehicles.

A very important step forward for the reduction of excess movement of freight during the period of fuel shortages was the introduction of the aforementioned Zonal scheme. Even though the story of the success of this project rightly belongs in the post-war period, there was a definite move towards reducing the number of goods stations handling small, uneconomic quantities of traffic by the late 1930s and the Railway Executive eliminated further waste on the grounds of economy. As a result more savings were brought about by the more intensive use of existing resources and the moratorium put on the replacement of horses by motors. The fleet strength at the end of 1939 was 2,473 motor vehicles of which 23 were jointly owned with the LMS or LNER railways. In addition a fleet of 2,176 trailers were in use, of which just 12 were jointly owned.

Even so, the armed forces continued to make what might be deemed as unrealistic demands on the railways such as: 'Can you deliver 50,000 tons of concrete to a mixing site on a new airfield at the rate of 400 tons per day?' Another task involved the GWR being asked to 'string out' all the pipes needed for a 150-mile pipeline running between the Bristol Channel and the South of England. Of course this was all on top of the existing traffics such as the supply of milk from the country areas to the dairies, the delivery of agricultural goods and the continuing replenishment of shelves in the village and town stores. To co-ordinate overall efficiency, a central board at headquarters handled the control of cartage operations during the war. They were responsible for ensuring that the flows of traffic were 'evened out' as far as possible with a number of 'float' vehicles held in reserve in strategic locations to help out at any trouble spots.

The major problems seemed to stem from the arrival of convoys of merchant ships, which brought huge volumes of goods into a given port (like Barry, Birkenhead, Bristol, Cardiff or Plymouth) en-mass. The ships had to be rapidly off-loaded and the goods dispersed to stores away from the dock areas, as these often came under nightly attack by the Luftwaffe. It therefore became the Cartage Controllers job to arrange movement of these 'float vehicles' to enable the convoys to be off-loaded in the shortest possible time.

It must also be noted that the GWR had to undertake other traffics that were substantially increasing in volume, especially in the supplies for the British, Commonwealth and American servicemen who were in transit camps awaiting the invasion of France. In this extra traffic we might look at the West Country as an example, for here the railways began to find a massive build up in goods moved by rail and road, or by road throughout, as the build up for D-Day began.

Above: *A Fordson model B takes broccoli to Marazion Station near Penzance for delivery by express goods train to London during World War II. To cope with seasonal growing spells the railway would often draft additional lorries into an area to handle the demand. At the time concerned, this lorry was shown as being allocated to Devonport depot at Plymouth. Presumably the broccoli load would be covered with sheeting for the journey.*
The late-David Cantrell Collection

Below: *This Bedford/Scammell OSS model is coupled to a tipping trailer named Jason F in telegraphic terms. The trailer is designed for the cartage of produce and has an unusual tailboard, designed to cause the least amount of damage to the load when discharging.*
Vauxhall Motors Ltd.

For example the volume of mail being sent to Devon and Cornwall increased dramatically as the 'invasion' forces moved down to their departure zones. At the same time foodstuffs, supplies and munitions were being carried in anything that could move. Between December 1943 and October 1944, the GWR moved no less than 156 motor vehicles, 123 horses and 225 trailers in to the two west country counties. Along with these went the crews required to operate these services, but four female 'carmen' were later to be returned home under a cloud having become pregnant and thus were unable to fulfil their duties. A memo was issued as a result of this, suggesting that only male carmen be allocated to areas where there were high concentrations of soldiers awaiting embarkation. In the months that followed June 1944, much use was made of the GWR road vehicle fleet in sustaining the forces fighting in Europe. Again food supplies and mail formed the bulk of the traffic. Yet all this traffic had an adverse effect, and all over the system, road vehicles were rapidly becoming worn out meeting the high demands on the service. It was with such a position that the GWR entered a new era of peace and its final two years of independence.

In reality the whole sphere of operation of road vehicles stood still during the war years, and overall the fleet size did not increase in comparison with the loads carried. The transfer from horse operation to motor vehicle still continued of course, but the shortages of new vehicles during the war limited the rate of change. Where it could be proved that motorising a service would increase its efficiency and help the war effort at the same time, progress was made, elsewhere things stood still or went backward. A number of rural services, motorised in the 1930s, saw their vehicles being whisked off elsewhere and replaced with horse drays. As peace resumed the number of vehicles required to bring the service back to strength were simply not available from the manufacturers, for the Government had urged Britain's motor companies to meet specific export quotas in order to bring in much needed foreign currency for the Exchequer. Steel and rubber shortages continued to hamper progress, and the austerity era did nothing to inspire things either. Meat, coal and bread were rationed even more severely than they had been during the war, but the politicians promised good times ahead.

Top Left: *We apologise for showing yet another Thornycroft Nippy tractor unit, but Bill has a certain fondness for them having part restored a similar unit and this photograph shows the Scammell trailer undercarriage quite clearly. The second and third photographs depict further Scammell automatic coupling tractors.*

Centre Left: *This is a 1946 Karrier Bantam tractor unit with a miniature version of the GWR safety cab. Due to post war shortages the vehicle was supplied with a spare wheel, but no tyre.*

Bottom Left: *This is the unusual Scammell MH3/6 model and featured the 3-ton coupling but had the 6-ton Mechanical Horse engine and was bought by the GWR for special duties.* BR Official

THE FINAL STAGE

The arrival of a new Labour government with many 'socialist' ideas, including state ownership of essential industries and services (coal, health, railways, docks and so on), set the scene for reconstruction. The debate over nationalisation of the railways had rumbled on from the end of World War I, and although the Big Four were distinctly opposed to the process, the reality of the national situation left little alternative. Senior officers in the Big Four all considered that a half-way step would be sufficient, and they wanted the Government to acquire the track, infrastructure and property holdings to create a national railway system akin to the national road system. Under this arrangement the companies would continue operating train services, and associated road operations, paying tolls for the facilities used.

Above: *One of the last vehicles to be supplied in GWR livery was this 1947 Thornycroft Nippy/Scammell 6-ton tractor unit.*

The compensation paid on the acquisition of the track and property would be invested in stock renewal, and improvements in services. However, this option was lightly dismissed as being impractical, although the John Major government achieved the very thing when it created Railtrack in the railway privatisation five decades later. Instead full nationalisation of railways, roads, docks, canals and airports was embarked upon, and a huge and unwieldy organisation was established. It is too great a story to cover in these remaining pages, nor does it really belong in a book on road vehicles, although it is partially told in our book on *British Railway Road Vehicles*. For the present, we must suffice by being simplistic about what happened to the railway road services in 1946 and 1947.

Above: *This Morris Commercial CV van, is seen during the 1950s in the British Railway livery of blood and custard (well carmine and cream to give it the official name). It has the luxury of a Swindon-built body designed for express parcels delivery. In using the word 'luxury, we do not do so idly' for this type of body was born from experience. It was high enough for the driver or his mate to stand up inside and there was direct access from the cab into the van body.*

Below: *This elderly Bedford/Scammell OSS tractor was actually ordered by the GWR, as part of a series of orders placed with the Luton factory between May 1944 and October 1947. It is seen here in later life delivering concrete bridge sections to one of the M4 Motorway construction sites in South Wales and thus placing yet another nail in the coffin of nationalised railways.* S. Vickery

Basically put, as far as the GWR were concerned, it was maintenance of the status quo. Road vehicles were bought (and in quite sizeable numbers), but in real terms these were merely replacements for worn-out or life-expired members of the fleet. Much greater use was made of 4-wheeled tractors fitted with auto-couplers and reasonably sized orders were placed with Karrier, Bedford and Thornycroft. A lot of new vehicles were allocated to the Country Lorry services, especially in food producing areas. The one significant increase in the fleet came with those vehicles allocated to the railhead scheme, where commercial pressures dictated the number of vehicles being operated. The well-known confectionery manufacturers Cadbury's alone requested that 50 new vehicles be introduced by early-1946 to cope with demand as sweet rationing was eased. However, whether this was an increase in the fleet or merely to return to their pre-war capacity is not known.

Other than this few real initiatives or innovations were possible, but in contrast with both the LMS and the LNER it can be stated the GWR were doing only the bare minimum. This can not have been down to the various shortages, because the other railways were getting around those problems, including the Southern who had a relatively small fleet of road vehicles. It may well be that the GWR's reticence to expand road services may well have been due to the threat of impending nationalisation. Even so the company did have one final fling with modern methods, as it began to widen the extent of the zonal goods scheme in those last years of independence - a subject that we have already covered in our book *British Railways Road Vehicles 1948-1968*.

A classic case of 'joint' development was seen in the movement of bulk traffic that expanded in the post-war period. The movement of goods in bulk was not new, but to the customer the practicality of receiving cement or china clay in anything but 1cwt. (50 Kgs) bags must have seemed very antiquated. The LMS, aware of the problem of getting large quantities of cement around the country, looked seriously at the creation of a special rail vehicle for the purpose. They came up with an idea to modify a steel grain wagon into a cement hopper, which could be loaded at the top and discharged at the bottom, even though it was not produced until after nationalisation. The GWR, along with the LMS and LNER, spent some time looking at road-rail containers for the conveyance of building materials. This was especially important during the reconstruction of Britain, when so much work was being done on replacement housing programmes and 'pre-fab' schemes.

As we have said, after the war the GWR attempted to update the vehicle fleet which, by 1945, was suffering from overwork and total lack of maintenance. In attempting to buy replacement vehicles the company was hampered by the lack of new trucks available for the home market since the by-word was export or die. Of the vehicles that were made available the company tried to obtain the largest size to cope with the increase in traffic and a number of 5- or 6-ton lorries like the Vulcan, Sentinel and Dennis entered the fleet as well as some Scammell Mechanical horses.

With the further introduction of Zonal schemes there was a need for a faster version of the Mechanical Horse to take the 6-ton articulated trailers between depots. Furthermore a sizeable quantity of four-wheeled Bedford and Thornycroft articulated tractor units were purchased with Scammell couplings. For the heavier indivisible loads that were hauled on low-loading trailers, a number of Foden timber tractors replaced some much earlier Foden steam waggons as well as some of the heavier duty tractors which were fitted with cabs for road use. The new Fodens came with 5- or 6-cylinder Gardner engines and many had winches and ground anchors fitted, it was a new beginning. But overhanging the Big Four, like the 'Sword of Damocles' was the threat of nationalisation, and as such money for improvements of any kind was strictly limited to 'as essentially required only'.

The GWR's road service, which had begun back in 1838, was now coming to an end and all future development would be subject to the whims of various political forces, as the railways became a state-owned entity. Innovations had been many and so many 'firsts' had been achieved, but one wonders how far it could have got had not two periods of World War and a slump in world trade intervened. In fact the GWR road services had faced many barriers during its 45-year life, both from external and internal forces. The major problem became competition from the often under-funded, but more efficient, road haulier. A major burden on all of the railway companies was that their charges had to represent, to a large extent, the cost of all of the fixed infrastructure assets such as track and signalling. The road haulier by contrast only had to pay a small fraction of the cost in maintaining the roads, as the bulk of the overhead was covered by the 'rates' received by local authorities. In fact the railway companies also paid rates and a portion of this money was also directed to maintaining roads, yet no one paid the railways to maintain their infrastructure.

The road hauliers were able to cream off the better paying traffic from the railways and even the acquisition of hauliers such as Pickfords, Hays Wharf and Carter Paterson did little to alleviate the problem. After World War I the Government did give the railway some recompense for the loss of earnings during the war, but it went nowhere to covering the enormous backlog of maintenance work required by a system abused and battered by six years of war. It did nothing at all to alleviate the lack of cash for new road vehicles. In fact it is to the companies credit that they were able to introduce new services at all during the inter-war period.

The introduction of the Road Traffic Act in 1933 gave the railways a brief respite, but in retrospect we can see that there was an official view that the railways were best at handling large quantities of regular traffic to specific destinations. This implies that the only worthwhile traffic was bulk train loads, but in fact the Contract Hire operation was ideal for the railway style of operation. In fact had the railways still retained their rail-fed town centre goods depots today and operated a 'break bulk' service for major companies as pioneered by the Great Western in the 1920s, then there would be less need for much of the trunking carried out on the motorways of today!

Above: *For a very long time all of the railway companies were involved in the transporting of complete agricultural shows or country fairs around the country during the summer. In all cases the most vital unit was the timber tractor, which used its winch to extract vehicles from the mud which usually accompanied the British summer. In this case an ex-GWR Foden DG is getting ready to rescue a Taylor mobile crane from the mire.* S. Vickery

Below: *The shortage of new vehicles after World War II meant that the railways had to buy whatever trucks were available. The Dennis company of Guildford had specialised in municipal vehicles for a long time, but the basic dustcart chassis was also a suitable base for a quality haulage vehicle that was ideal for railway work. As a consequence GWR ordered a batch of these 5-ton Dennis Pax chassis and gave them dropsides.* British Railways Western Region

As a conclusion to our Great Western Railway road vehicle book here is a GWR-designed Thornycroft Nippy at Cardiff in the mid-1950s. It is now looking well past its sell-by date, despite the small load, its unkempt BR maroon/cream livery shows signs of considerable use. One major design fault shows here: The wings supported the cab, but the wings themselves only gained support from the small quarter bumpers, which drooped, hence the cab tipped forward. S. Vickery

The next book in this series, covering the LMS (due to be published in October 2000), will examine the developments in replacing the horse on town cartage work and joint omnibus operations. The LNER book, due the following year will have more detail on the steam vehicles in use on that company's constituent members. The Southern Railway book will take a little while to prepare, because so little record remains of the railway road vehicle operations and even fewer photographs. Accordingly, from the outset of this book we would appeal to our readers to come forward with any information that they may have, no matter how large or small. In future books we aim to look at crew buses and engineering department vehicles, yet these vehicles were not that widely documented, so the help of our readers is actively sought. But for the meantime, we really do hope that you have enjoyed this book on **God's Wonderful Road Vehicles**.

With respect to this volume the authors would like to offer their sincere thanks to the following individuals and organisations who have done so much to help:-

G. Baker,	Mrs M. Cantrell
J. Coombes,	Cornish Railway Group,
the late J. Coiley	J. Cummins,
D. L. Davidson	A. A. Harrison
G. Lumb,	Mechanical Horse Club
G. Mustoe,	National Railway Museum
D. Sherer	Vauxhall Motors,
S. Vickery and	The Buckinghamshire Railway Society,

Could readers please note that due to the way in which the GWR allocated registration and fleet numbers conflicting dates and vehicle numbers have been found whilst researching this book and the authors have done their best to substantiate the information found within this small volume.